WORLD BANK WORKING PAPER NO. 108

Strategies for Cotton in West and Central Africa

Enhancing Competitiveness in the "Cotton-4"

Ilhem Baghdadli
Hela Cheikhrouhou
Gael Raballand

D1621653

THE WORLD BANK
Washington, D.C.

World Bank Working Papers are published to communicate the results of the Bank's work to the development community with the least possible delay. The manuscript of this paper therefore has not been prepared in accordance with the procedures appropriate to formally-edited texts. Some sources cited in this paper may be informal documents that are not readily available.

ISBN-10: 0-8213-7131-2   ISBN-13: 978-0-8213-7131-2
eISBN: 978-0-8213-7132-9
ISSN: 1726-5878   DOI: 10.1596/978-0-8213-7131-2

Ilhem Baghdadli is an Economist in the Africa Region Department at the World Bank. Hela Cheikhrouhou is a Financial Economist in the Latin America & Caribbean Region Department at the World Bank. Gael Raballand is a Transport Economist in the Africa Region Department at the World Bank.

Library of Congress Cataloging-in-Publication Data has been requested.

Contents

List of Tables

List of Figures

List of Boxes

Foreword

The cotton sector in WCA countries is an important contributor to growth, employment, and poverty reduction. In the late 1990s, the sector endured recurrent issues resulting in major underperformances, which called for actions and radical changes. Some countries embarked on cotton sector reforms, which meant breaking its vertically integration and increasing private sector participation. Other countries however have kept the structure of the industry almost intact.

The World Bank group has substantially supported these reforms and contributed extensively to documenting them. The World Bank maintains a strong interest in fostering cotton sector reforms as a way to improve its competitiveness and contribution to shared growth. The Bank considers case-by-case adaptation of industrial organization principles as essential for the design of further economic reforms and to increase effective involvement of private sector. Improving the competitiveness of the cotton sector in WCA countries is accordingly a critical part of the World Bank rural strategy in Africa and that of the Japanese Consultant Trust Fund, who contributed to funding consultancies that supported this work.

The present report can serve as a useful reference to policymakers in Benin, Burkina Faso, Chad, and Mali (the Cotton-4). Its main objective is to identify ways of enhancing competitiveness through sector reforms in these countries. The report promotes best practices to manage cost and define sales strategies so as to enhance the contribution of the cotton sector to shared growth and lessen the risk of contingent liabilities borne by the countries.

In publishing this report, we hope to provide an insightful analysis of the long-term opportunities in the WCA cotton sectors.

Francois Le Gall
Acting Sector Manager
Agriculture, Environment & Social Development
Central Africa

Acknowledgments

The main authors of this book are Ilhem Baghdadli, Hela Cheikhrouhou, and Gael Raballand. Other contributors are John Baffes, Virginie Briand, and Ndiame Diop.

The book was reviewed by Ronald Kopicki, Stephen Mink, and John Nash. The book also benefitted from inputs and comments from David Craig, John McIntire, Robert Blake, Joseph Baah-Dwomoh, Mary Barton Dock, Robert Robelus, Marc Sadler, Christophe Ravry, Olivier Durand, Edouardo Luis Leoa de Sousa, Luc Lecuit, Kristine Ivarsdotter, Amadou Konare, Delfin Sia Go, Michael Morris, Patrick Labaste, Ibrahim Nebie, Christopher Delgado, Chris Lane and Prosper Youm from IMF Mali, Wayne Camard from IMF Chad, Scott W. Rogers from IMF Burkina Faso, Lucien Humbert from AFD, Colin Poulton from Imperial College London, Joel Le Turionier (IFDC), Cristian Gaborel (IFDC), and Tom Bassett from University of Illinois.

The report also benefited from extensive interviews with European trading firms, namely Dagris, Copaco, Fimat, Devcot, Louis Dreyfus, Man Financial (namely Jérôme Jourquin), Econ Agroindustrial Corp. Ltd, Reinhart, Dunavant, Société Cotonnière de distribution S.A., Goenka-Impex S.A., Plexus, The Seam (namely Bill Ballenden), Cargill Cotton (namely Colin Iles), Cotton Outlook (namely Michael Edwards), Macquarie (namely Daryl French) and Icac (namely Gerald Esur).

Financial support was provided by the Japanese Consultant Trust Fund.

This work was performed under the overall leadership of Ilhem Baghdadli.

Acronyms and Abbreviations

ACC	Association Cotonnière Coloniale
AFD	Agence Française de Développement
AGAN	Agan Chemical Manufacturers limited
AIC	Association Interprofessionnelle du coton
BEC	Break Even Cost
BT	*Bacillus thuringiensis*
BACB	Banque agricole et commercial de Burkina
CAP	Common Agricultural Policy
CEDEAO	Communauté Economique des Etats de l'Afrique de l'Ouest
CFA	Communauté Financière Africaine
CFA F	Communauté Financière Africaine Franc
CFDT	Compagnie Française de Développement du Textile
CIPAM	Cooperativa Imprenditori Agricoli Meridionali Soc. Coop. a r.l
CMB	Cotton Marketing Board
CMDT	Compagnie Malienne de Développement des Textiles
Cotton-4	Benin, Burkina Faso, Chad, and Mali
DAC	Development Assistance Committee
EC	European Community
EU	European Union
FAO	Food and Agriculture Organization
FOB	Free On Board
GCCL	Ghana Cotton Company Limited
GDP	Gross Domestic Product
GIIF	Global Index Insurance Facility
GM	Genetically Modified
GPC	Groupement de Producteurs de Coton
HUICOMA	Huilerie Cotonnière du Mali
ICAC	International Cotton Advisory Committee
IER	Institut d'Economie Rurale
IFC	International Finance Corporation
IFDC	International Fertilizer Development Center
IMF	International Monetary Fund
IRCT	Institut de Recherche du Coton et des Textiles Exotiques
MIR	Regional Input Market (project of IFDC)
MRSC	Mission de Restructuration du Secteur Coton
MTM	Mark To Market
NYCE	New York Cotton Exchange
OECD	Organization for Economic Co-operation and Development
ONUDI	Organisation des Nations Unies pour le Développement Industriel
OTC	Over The Counter
PMG	Prix Minimum Garanti
ROE	Return On Equity
SAPHYTO	Société Africaine de Produits Phytosanitaires

SIDA	Swedish International cooperation Development Agency
SOAS	School of Oriental and African Studies
SOFITEX	Société des Fibres Textiles
SOFRECO	Société Française de Réalisation d'Etudes et de Conseil
SPIA	Société de produits industriels et agricoles
STEPC	Société Tropicale d'Engrais et de Produits Chimiques
TEU	Twenty-Foot Equivalent Unit
UEMOA	Union Economique et Monétaire Ouest Africaine
US$	United States Dollar
WCA	West and Central Africa
WAEMU	West Africa Economic and Monetary Union
WTO	World Trade Organization

Executive Summary

The cotton sector in WCA countries is very important in terms of its contribution to GDP and merchandise exports as well as poverty reduction. For example in Benin, Burkina Faso Chad and Mali, cotton's contribution to merchandise exports has ranged between 25 and 50 percent during the last few years, while its contribution to GDP is between 3 and 7 percent. Until recently, the cotton sector in most WCA countries was characterized by a vertically integrated monopolistic structure, whereby all transactions in the chain including, ginning, transportation and input supply were handled by the State Owned cotton company. Under this structure cotton production and exports grew considerably. For instance, in four countries (Benin, Burkina Faso, Chad and Mali) cotton production grew from 20,000 tons in 1960s to 600,000 tons in the mid 1990s.

However during the late 1990s, a number of internal and external factors created the need to reassess the structure of the cotton industries in the region. Internal factors included poor performances of the cotton companies, declining yields and poor extension services. External factors include downward trend in cotton price, with high volatility. This assessment revealed that, in this new context, vertically integrated monopolies were too costly an approach to ensuring vertical coordination of the cotton supply chain. Some countries embarked on cotton sector reforms, which meant breaking down the vertically integrated monopolies and increasing private sector participation. Other countries however have kept the structure of the industry almost intact.

The objective of this report is to identify ways of enhancing competitiveness through sector reforms in Benin, Burkina Faso, Chad, and Mali (the Cotton-4). The report promotes best practices to manage cost and define sales strategies so as to enhance the contribution of the cotton sector to shared growth and lessen the risk of contingent liabilities borne by the countries. Areas of improvement, investigated in the report, are associated with the following three targets: 1) increasing yields to produce larger volumes, 2) reducing cost and increasing the reliability of grading, and 3) enhancing sales revenues. The report also explains how these targets can be effectively pursued through sector reforms. Guidance is provided on the types of investors needed to improve the competitiveness of the cotton sector in WCA and ways to design privatization lots. The remaining of the Executive summary describes the key findings of the report.

Key Findings

Increasing Yields

Following impressive productivity gains during the 1960s and 1970s, cotton yields in WCA countries have stagnated since then. On the contrary, world average yields have increased by 1.8 percent per year. Therefore higher yields stand out as an important objective for WCA countries, which have no obvious niche market outlets and limited possibilities for diversification.

In addition to various exogenous factors, causes for yields stagnation include outdated technical practices, poor extension services, and input price. The report argues that increasing yields should come through strengthening research and extension as well as through reducing cost. The key recommendations of this section are the following:

- Clarify rules regarding how research and extension services are provided and are paid for.
- Update technical practices, including improvement of the fertilizer formula, which has been the same over the last thirty years and further development of integrated management program.
- Introduce sound regulatory framework, especially in relation to genetically-modified (GM) cotton.
- Improve input price setting mechanism (for example, as urea and NPKSB are priced at the same level, distributors have strong incentives to provide farmers with the cheaper urea when farmers would need the more expensive NPKSB).
- Remove procurement constraints. (For example, all input procurements enjoy supplier credit covering all need for a period of 240 to 270 days. This reduces competition between suppliers. The timing of the terms of references does not enable benefiting from the seasonality of fertilizer prices.)
- Harmonize all import tariffs for inputs (for example, insecticides are imported in end-user packaging and thus taxed at a higher rate than other input).

The area that must receive priority is making progress in GM cotton technologies, where Cotton-4 countries lag behind. Currently, more than one quarter of the area allocated to cotton is currently under GM varieties, accounting for almost 40 percent of world production. GM cotton in the UNITED STATES—where it was first introduced in 1996—currently accounts for about 80 percent of the area allocated to cotton. Other major GM cotton producers are Argentina (70 percent of cotton area), Australia (80 percent), China (60 percent), Colombia (35 percent), India (10 percent), Mexico (40 percent), and South Africa (90 percent). Countries that are at a trial stage include Brazil, Burkina Faso (the only SSA country), Israel, Pakistan, and Turkey. In Burkina Faso, significant research has been conducted to screen cotton varieties developed in other countries with the BT gene and see how well they perform in Burkina Faso's growing environment. However, Benin, Chad and Mali are still deliberating on whether or not to embrace GM technology.

Reducing Post-harvest Costs and Improving Quality

A second challenge to enhance competitiveness is reducing post-harvest costs and improving grading practices. It is a challenge because private companies have private information on their cost structure and no incentive to share it. Moreover, costs for doing the different activities along the chain are related by various risks—from "standard" commercial risks to hold-up risks. Reducing the costs of one activity along the supply chain may result in transferring risks to vertically-related activities, eventually increasing the costs of other activities (for example, reducing the costs for transport through outsourcing may result in increasing the cost for storage in the harbor). There are three areas, which the report argues needs to be improved: fiscal risk, transport cost and the reliability of grading.

Reducing fiscal risks would entail the following:

- Introducing more effective two-tier pricing mechanisms by setting initial price in the most prudent way regarding fiscal risk, and share profit, when campaigns end, by accurately reflecting market conditions.
- Ensuring consistency in the price mechanism to gain credibility and reputation.
- Promoting transparency through publication of annual reports by the companies and building mechanism to monitor costs.

Reducing transportation costs would entail that public Authorities concentrate on trade facilitation measures to reduce roadblocks costs and border-crossing costs. As for ginners, they should: be flexible when selecting ports; use medium term contracts to mitigate risk associated with transportation (both farm to gin and gin to export) and introduce the practice of ex-ginnery sales in addition to FOB ports sales.

The reliability of grading is also critical. Defects due to contamination of the lint cotton are imperceptible until the lint is processed by the textile industry. Given the speed with which the textile industry operates, it may be too late for the end-buyer, who as a result of inappropriate grading earlier in the supply chain will be unable to honor the contracts with the clothing industry. Since the price of lint cotton represents a very small portion of the costs incurred in making fabric, there is no incentive for buying cotton from risky origins. Achieving reliable grading is a goal that demands committed and continuous effort, and the benefits that accrue from it can vanish with just one year of unreliable grading.

Enhancing Sales Revenues

Volatility is an intrinsic characteristic of commodity markets, such as cotton. Consequently, poorly designed sales strategies that do not adequately manage price risk can undermine efforts to increase yields, improve cost structures, and enhance grading. Enhancing sales revenues must be a component of the global strategy to improve the competitiveness of the WCA cotton sector. In present day WCA, sales strategies are poor to non-existent, and this is a considerable source of inefficiency for the region's cotton sector. WCA ginners are supposed to be conservative in their sales management to secure their financial viability. Their noted absence of formal sales strategies and their "wait and see" attitude in peak market volatility periods may achieve just the opposite. For instance, for most of 2004 the €/US$ and the price of cotton experienced a downward trend, and WCA ginners remained absent from the market for several months hoping for a trend reversal, which is consistent with a speculative attitude. Moreover, a prolonged absence such as this can affect demand from spinners running out of supply of a specific origin.

A sound sales strategy should be based on protecting the breakeven cost, and either maximizing returns above it or minimizing losses below it, depending on market conditions. To do that, ginners must be able to analyze their cost structure in depth and carefully select their counterparts. They should also be able to use a wide range of available cotton contracts and adopt new sales techniques, such as on-line auctions, which have proven to boost sales revenues. In order to design and implement effective sales strategies, cotton companies need the capacity and incentives to behave pro-actively, which are lacking in most WCA countries—even when the sector had been partially privatized.

Table of Actions Needed to Improve the Competitiveness of the Cotton-4

Action needed	From	How could the World Bank help?	Urgency	Technical complexity
Improve Research and Extension				
Clarify rules regarding whose obligation it is to pay for the provision of Research and Extension (public sector Vs private sector). In the case of semi-public good, the terms of the public private partnerships must be articulated.	Governments of the Cotton-4, potential and actual investors	ESW are not compulsory but might help	High	Low
Update technical practices (e.g. the fertilizer formula has been the same for over 30 years; integrated management programs need to be further developed).	Research Institutes	IL, DPL	High	Low
Introduce sound regulatory framework, especially in relation to GM cotton.	Governments of the Cotton-4	ESW, IL, DPL	High	High
Reduce Input Costs				
Improve input price setting mechanism (e.g. As urea and NPKSB are priced at the same level, distributors have strong incentives to provide farmers with the cheaper urea when farmers would need the more expensive NPKSB)	Governments of the Cotton-4. Producers Distributors	ESW, training to strengthen producers capacities in IL, DPL	High	Medium
Remove procurement constraints (e.g. All input procurements enjoy supplier credit covering all need for a period of 240 to 270 days. This reduces competition between suppliers. The timing of the terms of references does not enable benefiting from the seasonality of fertilizer prices)	WAEMU, governments of the cotton 4	ESW	High	High
Revise tariffs nomenclature to have all input tariffs aligned (e.g. insecticides are imported in end-user packaging and thus taxed at a higher rate than other input)	WAEMU	DPL	Medium	Low
Improve input distribution.	Governments of the Cotton-4	ESW, IL	High	High
Reduce Costs and Unit Risks				
Introduce effective 2-tier pricing mechanism where needed and ensure its consistency over time	Governments of the Cotton-4, producers, ginners	ESW, DPL	High	Medium
Promote transparency through publication of annual reports by the companies	Governments of the Cotton-4, Ginners	DPL	High	Low

(Continued)

Table of Actions Needed to Improve the Competitiveness of the Cotton-4 (*Continued*)

Action needed	From	How could the World Bank help?	Urgency	Technical complexity
Reduce Costs and Unit Risks				
Build instruments to monitor costs	Governments of the Cotton-4, Ginners, Research Institutes	ESW, IL, DPL	High	Low
Reduce roadblocks costs and border-crossing costs	ECOWA, WAEMU, Governments of the Cotton-4,	DPL	High	High
Mitigate risks associated with transportation through medium term contracts and the introduction of ex-ginnery sales in addition to FOB port sales	Ginners	ESW	High	Low
Reduce transport costs through increased flexibility in the choice of ports	Ginners	ESW	Medium	Low
Improve the reliability of grading	WAEMU, Governments of the Cotton-4, Research institutes, producers, ginners, transporters.	ESW, IL, DPL	High	High
Cotton Price Risk Management				
Need an international exchange (e.g. NYCE, Euronext) to sponsor the new contract, with support from WAEMU, Governments of the cotton	Need an international exchange (e.g. NYCE, Euronext) to sponsor the new contract, with support from WAEMU, Governments of the Cotton-4, ginners	ESW, IL	High	High
Build the MIS tools and institutional capacity needed for proactive price risk management and sales strategy design/implementation	Ginners,	IL	High	High
Identify how seed-cotton pricing scheme should influence sales strategies	Ginners, Governments of the Cotton-4,	ESW	High	Low
Diversify sales through on-line auctioning	Ginners	ESW, DPL	Medium	Low

(*Continued*)

Table of Actions Needed to Improve the Competitiveness of the Cotton-4 (*Continued*)

Action needed	From	How could the World Bank help?	Urgency	Technical complexity
Support Competitiveness Through Cotton Sector Reform				
Design privatization lots	Mali, Chad	ESW	High	Low
Specify the types of investors needed along the chain	Mali, Chad	ESW	High	Low
Improve business climate to attract best available investors and maximize their willingness to pay to own a piece of the market	WAEMU, Governments of the Cotton-4,	ESW	High	High

Privatization will not cure poor sales management and subsequent fiscal risk unless governments design privatization schemes to attract solid, long-term investors. If the government decides to privatize, it may wish to target international strategic investors (rather than local investors, for instance), who have the expertise and financial muscle to deal with intra-seasonal and inter-seasonal volatility. In addition, these investors will introduce best international practices to sales management, provided the government establishes the right incentives.

Governments should continue to push for the creation of a World Cotton Futures contract. Financial markets are incomplete, as they do not currently provide perfect hedging instruments for non-U.S. cotton. However, the increasing volume of exported non-U.S. cotton provides hope for the successful development of a world cotton future contract.

Promoting Competitiveness Through Sector Reforms

Lessons learned from the 1990s suggest that transferring public property to private enterprises is not enough, by itself, to put the sector back to a sustainable path, Policy reforms in cotton sectors should not only consist of making the decision to privatize, they should be consistent with the following process:

- Restructure the market by identifying what market structure should replace the vertically integrated monopoly,
- Deregulate the industry by articulating how to go from public monopoly to the new market setting (strengthen competition law and build contracting devices and capacities, while removing regulations), and
- Implement a privatization scheme to actually transfer some or all the property rights of the monopoly to the private sector.

The report argues that IO criteria can be effective tools to compare privatization options and design reforms to best implement privatization scheme. Based on these criteria, the report gives some guidance on the types of investors needed to improve the competitiveness of the cotton sector in WCA as well as ways to design privatization lots. However, further research would be needed to turn these findings into country specific policy reform agenda.

CHAPTER 1

The Cotton Sector in West and Central Africa: A Success Story with Challenges Ahead

John Baffes and Ilhem Baghdadli

Following decades of development efforts, cotton became the dominant cash crop in most WCA countries, including Benin, Burkina Faso, Chad and Mali, referred to as the "Cotton-4" in the rest of this report. Apart from good agro-climatic conditions, the increase in cotton production reflected the vertically-integrated structure of the cotton sector—which was similar in many cotton producing countries—and hence the avoidance of free riding risks that would have otherwise jeopardized the viability of the sector.

Despite the success, the changing nature of the external environment, including the downward trend and volatile nature in world prices along with inefficiencies of the state-owned cotton companies called into question the effectiveness of the vertically-integrated structure of the cotton. As a consequence, after the mid-1990s the governments of the Cotton-4 began reassessing the rationality of the existing structure of the cotton sector. Furthermore, following the price declines of the late-1990s, fiscal transfers from state budgets to cotton companies grew considerably putting into jeopardy the fiscal position of these countries. With financial and technical assistance from the donor community and especially the World Bank and the IMF, Governments of the Cotton-4 contemplated policy reforms in order to bring the cotton sector back to a sustainable path and, ultimately, increase the welfare of cotton growers.

This chapter reviews the global economic and policy environment against which policy reforms in the Cotton-4 countries must be undertaken as well as the domestic impediments that the sector faces. Issues of global nature include the declining and volatile nature of cotton prices, exchange rates, and OECD cotton subsidies. Key domestic issues include the sluggish adjustment of producer prices and the poor management of cotton companies. The chapter also reviews the types of reforms instituted in the Cotton-4 countries and gives a broad outline of further actions.

Table 1. Cotton's Importance to Cotton-4 (2001–03 Averages)

	Benin	Burkina Faso	Chad	Mali
Value of cotton export ($ million)	126	105	53	193
Cotton's export share (%)	27.7	44.6	29.4	22.7
Cotton's contribution to GDP (%)	4.5	3.3	2.4	6.1
Merchandise exports ($ million)	455	235	182	849
Per capita income (US$200)	289	245	381	203
Cotton area (hectares)	310,267	560,000	273,750	553,223
Cotton yield (kg/hectare)	1,378	1,150	700	1,042
Number of ginneries	18	14	9	17

Source: Food and Agriculture Organization (FAOSTAT) and World Bank (World Development Indicators), and various country sources.

Why Reform a Growing Sector?

Following independence, the political leadership of most countries supported a variety of actions aimed at boosting cotton production. Since then, cotton has become one of the primary sources of cash in the Cotton-4. For example, cotton's contribution to merchandize exports of these countries ranges between 23 and 45 percent while its contribution to GDP ranges between 2.5 and 6 percent (see Table 1). During the early 1960s, the Cotton-4 produced 20,000 tons of cotton lint. Within a 20-year period, cotton production increased 7-fold, with the exception of Chad where production increased by about 50 percent. From an insignificant cotton producing region during the 1960, WCA countries exceeded one million tons of cotton lint in 2005, accounting for 4.3 percent of global output and 13 percent of global exports, the third larger cotton exporter after the United States and Central Asia.

Often, the production increase was stimulated by the donor community, especially the World Bank, which during the 1980s offered significant financial assistance to the Cotton-4. For instance, the West Volta Cotton Project in Burkina Faso and the Borgou Rural Development project in Benin successfully aided these countries to significantly expand the areas under cotton as well as enhance their yields. In the Cotton-4, production increased from 150,000 tons of cotton lint in the early 1980s to about 700,000 during the last few years (see Figure 1).

However, numerous exogenous and endogenous factors precipitated the reform of the cotton sector. Key domestic factors are: (i) prices received by producers have been low, even after allowing for all transaction costs; (ii) inflexibility of the panterritorial pricing mechanism, which effectively transferred resources from efficient producers to inefficient ones—in effect playing the role of a poorly designed and executed poverty reduction strategy; (iii) high degree of corruption of the cotton companies, which in the name of price stabilization objectives taxed producers in periods of high prices only to be unable to compensate them in periods of low prices; (iv) inflexibility of the input supply mechanisms which only allowed inputs to be used for cotton thus imposing a constraint on diversification; and (v) low profitability due to stagnating yields.

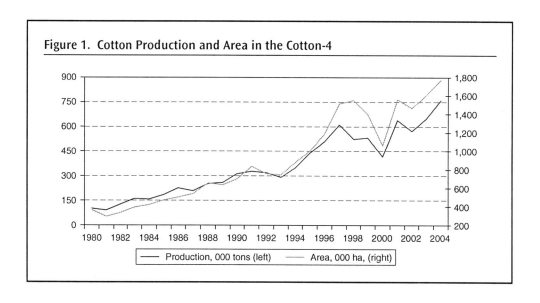

Figure 1. Cotton Production and Area in the Cotton-4

Adjusting to Exogenous Factors

Volatile prices, which are low and follow a downward trend, give rise to the "cotton problem" in countries that are highly dependent on that crop, such as Benin, Burkina Faso, Chad and Mali.

High Volatility. The degree of price volatility for cotton has been high during the last four decades and spiked in the period from 1973–1984. Baffes (2005) shows that world cotton prices were over three times more volatile during 1973–1984 than during 1960–1972 and at least twice as volatile during 1985–2002 as during the initial period. Valdes and Foster (2003) found similar results for price variability of corn, rice, sugar, and wheat, and Sarris (2000) for wheat and maize. On the other hand, Gilbert (2006) ranked 21 commodities according to their volatility and found cotton to be in the middle. Given that most commodity prices are just as volatile as cotton prices (and most prices have a tendency to move together), producing multiple cash crops may be a desirable diversification strategy but would not significantly reduce risk.

Declining Prices. Not only have international market prices for cotton been volatile, they have been declining. For example, between 1960–64 and 1999–2003 real cotton prices fell 55 percent, in line with the 50 percent decline in the broad agriculture price index of 22 primary commodities (see Figure 2). Reasons for such decline include reduced production costs, resulting from technological improvements on the supply side, stagnant per capita consumption, and competition from synthetic products which currently account for about 40 percent of total fiber consumption (down from 65 percent in the early 1960s). Reductions in production costs have been associated primarily with yield increases (world average), from 300 kilograms per hectare in the early 1960s to about 700 kilograms per hectare in 2005. This yield increase reflects the introduction of improved varieties and increased use of irrigation and chemical fertilizers. Furthermore, the spread of genetically modified seed

Table 2. Global Balance of the Cotton Market (Thousand Tons)

	1960	1970	1980	1990	2000	2002	2004	2005
PRODUCTION								
China	1,372	1,995	2,707	4,508	4,417	4,916	6,320	5,769
United States	3,147	2,219	2,422	3,376	3,818	3,747	5,062	4,946
India	1,012	909	1,322	1,989	2,380	2,312	4,080	4,250
Pakistan	306	543	714	1,638	1,816	1,736	2,482	2,309
Central Asia	1,491	2,342	2,661	2,593	1,412	1,509	1,737	1,724
Brazil	425	549	623	717	939	848	1,318	1,207
Franc Zone	63	140	224	562	728	952	1,135	1,071
Turkey	192	400	500	655	880	900	900	805
Australia	2	19	99	433	804	386	624	497
Greece	63	110	115	213	421	375	390	380
World	10,201	11,740	13,831	18,970	19,437	19,437	26,193	24,958
EXPORTS								
United States	1,444	848	1,290	1,697	1,472	2,591	3,000	3,215
Central Asia	381	553	876	1,835	1,203	1,172	1,251	1,316
Franc Zone	48	137	185	498	767	833	952	1,092
Australia	0	4	53	329	849	575	420	561
Brazil	152	220	21	167	68	170	360	425
Greece	33	0	13	86	244	275	263	283
India	53	34	140	255	24	17	175	275
Syria	97	134	71	91	212	120	152	150
Egypt	346	304	162	18	79	150	140	125
Tanzania	34	66	36	40	39	41	88	99
World	3,067	3,875	4,414	5,081	5,857	6,618	7,542	8,270

Notes: Bangladesh is included in Pakistan prior to (and including) 1970. Franc Zone includes Benin, Burkina Faso, Cameroon, Central Africa Republic, Chad, Côte d'Ivoire, Guinea-Bissau, Madagascar, Mali, Niger, Senegal, and Togo. Central Asia includes Uzbekistan, Turkmenistan, Tajikistan, Kazakhstan, Azerbaijan, and Kyrgyzstan.
Source: International Cotton Advisory Committee, *Cotton: Review of the World Situation,* various issues.

technology in developing countries and precision farming in developed countries is expected to reduce the costs of production even further.

In the Cotton-4, rise in production was made possible by a dramatic enlargement of cultivated areas. This increase came from both substitutions in cotton areas to other crops and additions that have expanded total cultivated areas. Such increase has been managed poorly. As a result, soils are dramatically depleted and nutrient-poor, which translates into a diminished capacity to absorb rainfall and further loss of organic matter. Furthermore, newly cultivated areas are not always in the most favorable zones for cotton production. Yields per hectare are low and prospects for improvement are quite limited

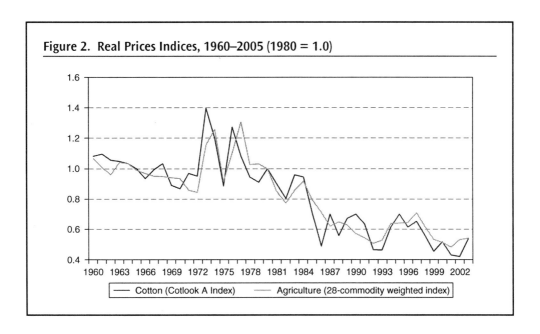

Figure 2. Real Prices Indices, 1960–2005 (1980 = 1.0)

for a variety of reasons, including the fact that these zones are poorly equipped with little infrastructure.

The Exchange Rate. Cotton is traded in U.S. dollars, as most primary commodities are. Thus, the exchange rate plays a fundamental role in the competitiveness of the Cotton-4. The inflexibility of the exchange rate regime sometimes exacerbates movements in world prices. The world price for cotton, the Cotlook Index A, has clearly been characterized by large annual fluctuations over the last 24 years. For instance, the 1994 CFA F devaluation (from 50 to 100 CFA F per FF) coincided with a large upturn in world market prices, which together resulted in 189 percent nominal rise increase in the CFA F price of cotton. On the other hand, the appreciation of the U.S. dollar relative to the euro partially moderated the 52 percent drop in cotton prices in the CFA zone between 1995 and 2002. The sharp decline of world prices in 2001 and 2002 could therefore have been more damaging had the dollar not been appreciating vis-à-vis the euro. However, Cotton-4 producers were not able to reap the benefits of post-2002 cotton price increase due to the euro's appreciation.

Assistance to Cotton Producers in OECD Countries. To make matters worse, the global cotton market has been subject to numerous market and trade interventions, which appear to have exacerbated the decline (and, perhaps, volatility) of international cotton prices. The International Cotton Advisory Committee (ICAC 2002), which has been monitoring assistance to cotton production since 1997, finds that at least eight countries have consistently supported cotton production: Brazil, China, Egypt, Greece, Mexico, Spain, Turkey, and the United States. The United States (world's sector largest producer and largest exporter), the EU, and (to a lesser extent) China, however, are the largest subsidizers (see Table 3). The subsidies, which reached an estimated $6 billion in 2001, coincided with record low prices—not surprisingly since the two are negatively correlated by design—caused two

Table 3. Estimated Government Assistance to Cotton Producers, 1997–2004 (US$ Millions)

	1998	1999	2000	2001	2002	2003	2004
U.S.	1,132	1,882	3,809	1,868	3,307	2,889	1,372
China	2,648	1,534	1,900	1,217	800	1,303	1,145
Greece	660	596	537	735	718	761	836
Spain	204	199	179	245	239	233	230

Source: International Cotton Advisory Committee; U.S. Department of Agriculture; European Union.

major reactions. First, Brazil initiated a WTO consultation arguing that (i) U.S. export subsidies are illegal and (ii) the level of subsidies is so high that it depresses world prices, and (iii) some of the U.S. subsidies have been inappropriately declared as non-trade distorting in the WTO. The WTO dispute panel largely decided in favor of Brazil. Second, the Cotton-4 made a proposal to the WTO requesting the removal of cotton subsidies by OECD countries–the so-called cotton initiative in favor of cotton- and until such removal takes place, they should be compensated accordingly. Both the WTO outcome on the Brazil/U.S. dispute and the cotton initiative figured prominently during the sixth WTO ministerial in Hong Kong (see Appendix B for the cotton initiative and the Hong Kong ministerial).

The effect of subsidies on world cotton prices and the export share of WCA cotton producers has been a highly debated and controversial subject. However, that taking an average of all models that simulated the impact of subsidies, gives an effect in the order of 10 to 15 percent, that is, that OECD subsidies depress world cotton prices by about 10 to 15 percent (see discussion in Appendix A). This would be consistent with about $150 million of losses to WCA countries. In terms of the likely outcomes in response to the Doha Development Agenda, the EU's decision to decouple support to its cotton sector, the recent U.S. decision to remove export subsidies, and perhaps some more reduction in domestic support by the United States, it appears that world cotton prices may restore one third of their losses due to subsidies.

Addressing Endogenous Weaknesses

Following decades of expansion, the long-term competitiveness of the WCA cotton sector is called into question as productivity and efficiency decline while other more productive producers expand their market share (e.g. Brazil). Without further domestic reforms, the sector can no longer be the major stimulus for growth and poverty reduction. Indeed, even if the world market conditions become more favorable, either in response to reduction of OECD subsidies, demand stimulus, or some supply constrains, it is likely that the most-efficient cotton producers will increase their volumes of production, thereby preventing the Cotton-4 to increase their share in the world market. Hence, striving to improve competitiveness and preparedness through domestic reforms should be a priority (in addition to demanding removal of OECD subsidies).

Cotton sector reforms, which mostly consist of reducing the public sector's role in the cotton sector, are aimed at favoring the highest contribution possible to shared and sustainable economic growth. These targets were supposed to be met through the creation of a business climate to the development, distribution, and adoption by producers of new technologies. These technologies should help make productivity gains. Most needs in the subregion's cotton sector relate to: 1–seed breeding and the introduction of new varieties, with higher yield potential and ginning out-turn ratio, and 2–improving soil fertility by designing and implementing the best research and extension agendas, strengthening the mechanization of soil preparation, developing more irrigation projects and enhancing harvest techniques. Enabling the Cotton-4 to have access to these technologies and the know-how needed to best stimulate market efficiency and welfare is the cornerstone of the reform process underway in WCA.

The Sluggish Adjustment of Producer Prices. Since elaborate sales conditions detract from the value and attractiveness of an enterprise, and may undermine a privatization deal (Welch and Fremond 1998), pre-privatization sector reforms are supposed to fix price controls and other problem areas as early as possible. Indeed, seed cotton pricing schemes assure potential investors of doing stable business in a transparent manner. The more transparent the pricing scheme, the better a potential investor can calculate possible returns on investment. When expected returns are clear, potential investors are relatively willing to pay to enter the market. Moreover, sound rules for setting producers' prices help screen for good investors, that is, investors who have the potential to develop the cotton sector in an effective and sustainable manner. These are the reasons the design and implementation of seed cotton pricing schemes has been such an important part of sector reform supported by the World Bank.

Despite efforts to identify and implement a sound pricing scheme in the Cotton-4, producers' prices appear to not have been related to international cotton prices. Econometric evidence suggests that there is little contemporaneous co-movement between the "A Index" and prices received by producers in the Cotton-4 countries. The share of the "A Index" received by cotton growers has, however, significantly increased from its levels in the 1980s. In the early 1980s, producers' share of international prices was 35 percent in Benin, 28 percent in Burkina Faso, 30 percent in Chad and 31 percent in Mali. The Governments of the Cotton-4 took advantage of the devaluation of the CFA franc and the simultaneous increase in the U.S. dollar world price to shrewdly manage producer prices and increase the overall profitability of the sector in the nineties. This prudent stance has been reversed in the first four seasons of the millennium, where the share of producers in the world price averaged 60 percent in Benin, 58 percent in Burkina Faso, 48 percent in Chad and 61 percent in Mali, with producer prices maintained at a relatively high level against a spectacular decline in international prices.

The Financial Health of the Sector's Historic Operators. The effects on the sector's financial health from the relative insensitivity of producer prices to world prices were compounded by serious mismanagement of profits from the lucrative years following the devaluation of the CFA franc. In Mali, for instance, the CMDT was in no position to manage the downturn in international prices in 1997–98, primarily because of poor management decisions. The stabilization fund, created to set aside a portion of profits from the year of high prices, turned

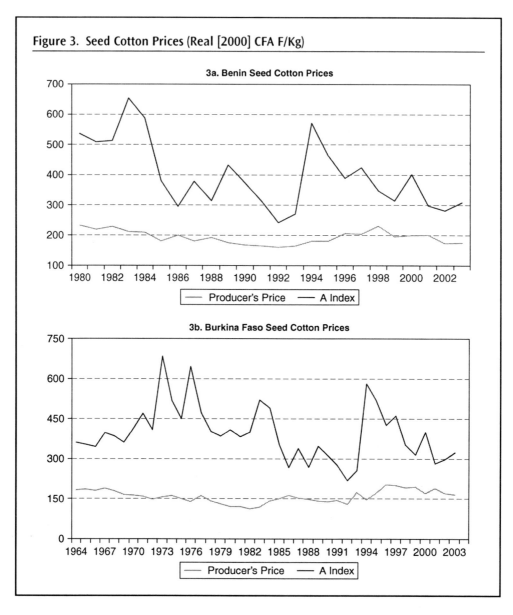

Figure 3. Seed Cotton Prices (Real [2000] CFA F/Kg)

out to be empty when price declined resulting in a heavy financial loss of CFA F 56 billion ($100 million), prompting a new bailout of CMDT. These factors have deeply undermined farmer confidence in the system. The farmers decided to reduce cotton planting when producer prices were reduced to CFA F170 in 2000–01 leading to a 50 percent decline in cotton production. When the following year CMDT agreed to a higher producer price, while to increase in production, the continued decline in world market prices accentuated the company's financial difficulties. While SOFITEX, in Burkina Faso, has been the best performer of the subregion over the last few years, the company likewise encountered a number of pitfalls in managing its stabilization fund. For instance, the endowments of the stabilization fund were not used to smooth over inter-seasonal volatility but rather to finance fertilizers and pay for non-provisioned bonuses. The price mechanism in Burkina Faso implies the payment of

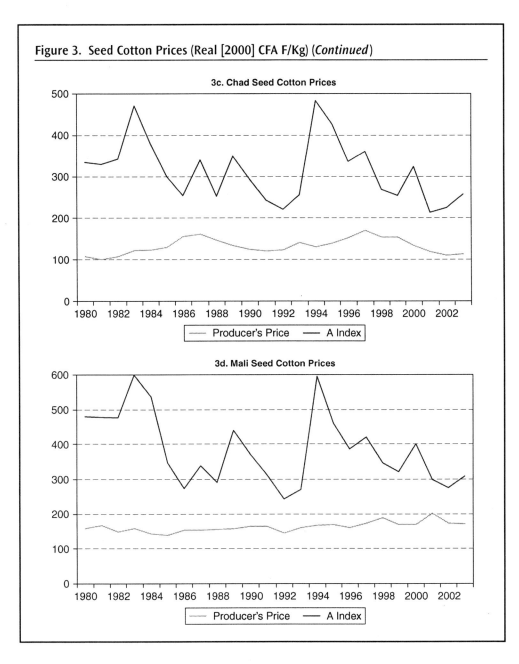

Figure 3. Seed Cotton Prices (Real [2000] CFA F/Kg) (*Continued*)

next year's bonus is based on the profitability situation of the current year. Yet, the agreements made by the company and the producers to use the fund to pay for deliberate errors in estimates of the profits provided incentives for mismanagement. The reform efforts in the cotton sectors of WCA countries were meant to prevent such outcomes.

What Types of Reforms Were Instituted?

While cotton sector reforms throughout the region shared the same goals, the processes to reach them varied from country to country.

Benin

The reforms in Benin, which were done 'by function', consisted of two key elements: (i) separation of the various links in the cotton supply chain according to the different functions (input provision and distribution, seed cotton production, transport, ginning and trading); (ii) division of the responsibility for handling these functions among a large number of actors—except for research and extension, which was considered a semi-public good that needed to be jointly funded by the private and public interests at stake; and (iii) organize the main decision making process, such as price setting, cotton delivery time, etc. into horizontally organized entities, which must all agree before the final decision is made (through the Association Interprofessionnelle du Coton). Every segment of the supply chain was thus opened to different types of investors.

Burkina Faso

The reform process in Burkina Faso was performed "by region," in a sense reflecting the view that free riding risks of the cotton sector are high, especially with regards to the provision of inputs and research & extension. The privatization scheme assumed that investors will be active all along the chain and guarantee payment for cotton research activities, extension services, seed cotton purchase, ginning and trading. The market is currently structured into three regional monopolies (a dominant company SOFITEX, accounting for about 85 percent of cotton, with two competitive fringe companies, namely Socoma and Faso Coton). Unlike Benin, this scheme targeted international strategic investors willing to undertake (and manage) risk and enough capital base to continue funding research and extension services.

Chad

Progress on cotton reforms in Chad has been somewhat limited by the fiscal difficulties of Cotontchad (the publicly-owned company that handles all cotton-related marketing transactions), and the lack of ownership of reform by the government. Although the government of Chad had decided to disengage from the cotton sector in 1999, so far it has failed to take the necessary steps to move in this direction.

Mali

The Government of Mali reconsidered its reform commitment in July 2004, in effect arguing that the Malian cotton sector should be reformed along the lines of Burkina Faso's, rather than Benin. In November 2005, the government increased its share in the capital of the cotton monopsony (from 60 to 70 percent).

What is the Way Forward? Towards a Competitiveness Approach

Governments of the Cotton-4 need to provide the right incentives to enhance the competitiveness of their cotton sectors. Enhancing the competitiveness of the cotton sector can

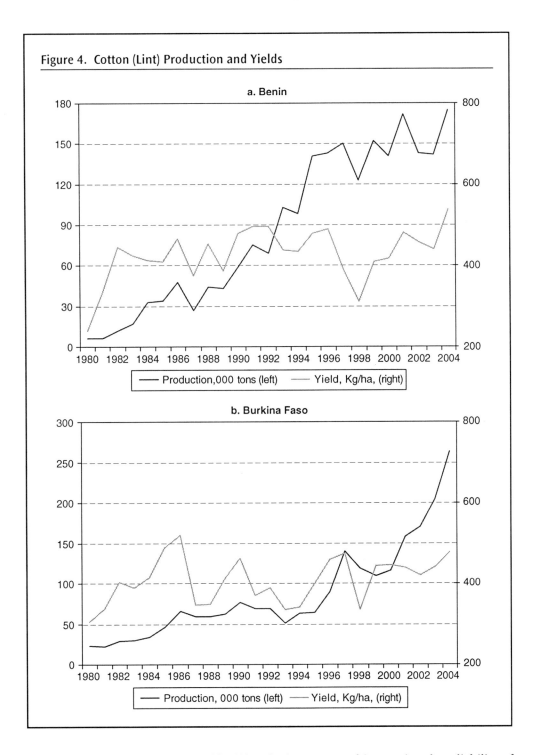

Figure 4. Cotton (Lint) Production and Yields

a. Benin

b. Burkina Faso

be achieved by: (i) increasing yields, (ii) reducing costs and improving the reliability of grading, (iii) enhancing sales revenues, and (iv) introducing a superior market structure and organization. The following four sections summarize the findings on each of these approaches.

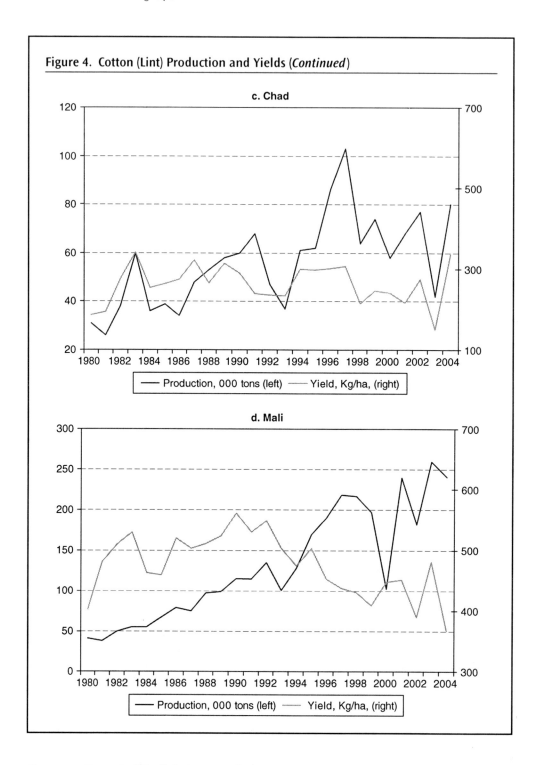

Figure 4. Cotton (Lint) Production and Yields (*Continued*)

From an Expected Deficit Approach . . .

The World Bank's support to the cotton sector of WCA countries has been based on the expected deficit approach (or *ex ante* equilibrium). This approach relies on the actual financial performance of the industry to define the magnitude of external support, if any, that would be needed to balance—at the very least—cotton costs and revenues. This approach, however, assumes that the cost structure and revenues associated with each step of cotton production is common knowledge. However, given high price volatility and unpredictable growing conditions, it is impossible to make accurate price and quantity forecasts required to determine the company's deficit.

An *ex ante* equilibrium approach can be useful to estimate worst case scenarios for sales prices, because it is usually based on "conservative" deficit estimates that use market lows. However, the approach is not providing an effective proxy for the sector's real performance, and can even lead to moral hazard, as the objective becomes to maximize donor support.[1] The ultimate objective should be to minimize the risk to the government of contingent liabilities due to poor performance from the cotton sector. As such, the best available options of cotton price risk management have to be considered when evaluating deficits. However, the current approach is not providing an effective proxy for the sector's real performance. Ginneries in the Cotton-4, for example, do not make their balance sheet publicly available, so their actual performance is unknown. Therefore, policymakers and donors usually derive their own estimates of the sector's performance.

The shareholders and creditors probably do require independent annual audits, which would certify that the financial statements are in line with accounting standards, but these would not make a judgment on the quality of cost and revenue management. Such annual audit reports and financial statements give a general picture of the financial health of the ginner at one point in time, but cannot provide an analysis of the performance of sales management. The current approach by donors and governments consists of evaluating the performance of the cotton industry per season. This means that the objective is to estimate the volume produced per season, the sales revenues per season and the costs incurred per season. This is very tricky to determine since cotton seasons overlap each other. As Box 1 illustrates, when ginning companies prepare their financial statements at the close of the calendar year, their annual net income reflects a mixture of events and does not provide information on the deficit or surplus of the cotton season.

. . . to a Competitiveness Approach

The competitiveness approach consists of promoting best practices to manage costs and define sales strategies. It does not assume that the cotton supply chain and its revenues are common knowledge but sets targets for cost reductions or increases in revenues for the future, thereby resulting in an improved financial performance. Specifically, its objective is to improve the financial performance of the company and hence lessen the risk of contingent liabilities borne by the countries. Practically, this may translate into minimizing deficits or maximizing profits. The approach is thus different from the equilibrium approach, which

---

1. Example: As mentioned in the Implementation Completion Report on the third Structural Adjustment Credit for Mali, the short-term action plan supported by the project had 4 elements, including an emergency financial rescue plan for the cotton parastatal, the CMDT that covered the company's cash deficit and the projected operational loss for the 2001–2002 season. (See report No. 29606-MLI–2004)

Box 1: Cotton Marketing Calendar, 2005/06 Season

1st Quarter 2004: Forward sales start for shipment Jan–Dec. 2005 (n principle, ginning 2003–04 crop ends May/June 2004).

Mid-2004: Ginning companies order and purchase inputs (fertilizers, insecticides, some herbicides) for 2005 (credit from input suppliers).

November 2004–May 2005: Inputs distributed to farmers (during purchase of ginning of 2004–05 crop, including seeds, one-year credit, no payment up front).

1st quarter 2005: Forward sales start for shipment Jan–Dec 2006.

March/May 2005: Producer price and input prices announced before planting.

June-early–July 2005: Planting.

August–mid-September-2005: Crop financing negotiated with Banks (local and international), using forward sales contracts (with international banks) or stocks (with national banks) as collateral.

November 2005–April 2006: Seed cotton purchases from farmers, recovery of input credit, ginning.

December 2005–December 2006: Export shipments.

November 2005–May 2006: When applicable, payment of a bonus to producers.

---

though better in some ways, fails to be practicable under present circumstances and carries with it moral hazard risks. Unlike the equilibrium approach, the competitiveness approach can be defined by policymakers *ex-ante* and can benefit the industry's actual performance. This approach is at the core of the analysis in the rest of this report.

CHAPTER 2

Increasing Yields

Ilhem Baghdadli and Virginie Briand

Increasing yields stands out as an important objective for WCA, among the very few options for restoring cotton's contribution to shared growth in the subregion. Cotton will be able to make a contribution to growth in the Cotton-4 only if its production remains competitive in global market. Assuming no differences in quality, competitiveness will depend on yields, unit costs and sale prices. In some cases competitiveness can be maintained or increased even in the face of falling yields. In the case of WCA cotton production, efforts must be sought on all fronts (Chapter 3 deals with costs and chapter 4 with sales revenues).

Increasing yields is also made important by the fact that there is no obvious niche-market, where significant volumes of WCA cotton could be traded at a higher price than market average. Ongoing experiences aimed at developing fair trade and organic cotton show that options for getting a better return exist but concern small volumes and can not be scaled up so as to solve the "cotton problem." Thus, increasing yields and/or lowering the total cost of production are the only credible ways of sustaining cotton revenues. There are physical limits to increasing volumes, not to mention negative externalities having to do with soil fertility and the environment. Consequently, increased yields are vital to the success of the sector in WCA, and all factors that could help lead to that outcome should be carefully considered.

Lessons learned from past experiences suggest three factors are responsible for yield stagnation: 1–exogenous factors, 2–the design of technical practices and extension services, and the lack of incentives for producers to carry out technical recommendations; 3–the cost for input. The quality of technical practices might be improved through the introduction of enhanced cotton varieties, larger diffusion of animal traction, and better use of inputs. Identifying the appropriate incentives to carry out sound technical recommendation is essential in preventing poor economic optimization. Improving input distribution might be needed to reduce input cost.

Why Do Seed Cotton Yields Matter?

Yield stagnation is neither unique to WCA nor a new phenomenon. Fock (1998) underlines that until the Great Depression, cotton production increased in the United States, despite stagnating yields. Worldwide, yields have sharply increased since the early sixties. However, this global rise in yields has not been stable, but rather has been marked by multiple stagnations and recoveries. As for WCA, Figure below shows that seed cotton yields have evolved according to different patterns within the Cotton-4. While the evolution of yields in Benin is atypical and must be analyzed with caution, improvements in the other three countries' yields have often been followed by commensurate drops. Interestingly, the increase in production remains steady over the period in these three countries. Yields improved significantly during the late 1970s and the early 1980s but have stagnated since then, albeit major cotton sector reforms.

In certain situations (niche markets) it may not be critical to achieve relatively high yield levels. When there are opportunities for niche sales in market segments where competitiveness is not defined solely by cost-effectiveness, increasing yields becomes less important. Conversely, stagnating yields are problematic for product that cannot be sold to niche markets, where low yields and volumes may be compensated for by high margins. For a commodity such as cotton, fair trade and organic markets provide high premium sales options. However, pilot experiences strongly suggest that these options cannot be scaled up in such a way as to solve the "cotton problem" (see Box 2 for a description of ongoing experiences). Thus, generally speaking, volume matters and—because extension of cultivated areas confronts physical limits and causes negative externalities—yield matters.

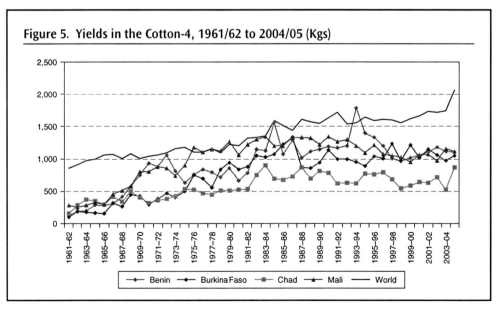

Figure 5. Yields in the Cotton-4, 1961/62 to 2004/05 (Kgs)

Source: FAOSTAT, 2005.

Box 2: Niche Markets: Organic and Fair Trade Cotton

Programs of organic and/or fair trade cotton are under preparation in the subregion with the idea of supplying already identified target markets in some European countries. Despite their benefits and popularity among small producers, these programs are not without obstacles. The main challenges have to do with the current scope of opportunities, the costs of production supervision, and the absence of a local textile industry.

For the last four years, Helvetas has been implementing a program aimed at supplying 5 percent of the Swiss textile market with Malian fair trade organic cotton by 2007/08. A similar program has been launched in Burkina Faso. Recently, Dagris, the French company started supporting a program of fair trade cotton.

Organic fair trade cotton programs are very popular among small producers for several reasons. By definition, organic cotton programs exclude the use of chemical fertilizers or pesticides and thus circumvent the problem of accessing input credit. Furthermore, these programs take place on small lots (from 0.25 to 0.5 hectares) that can be cultivated by women (45 percent of organic cotton producers are female) in addition to their chores, or by any other family member willing to get some revenue that he/she cannot earn through family farming (which provides for his/her essential needs such as food and clothing, but is not paid labor). Besides, organic and fair trade cotton benefits from a higher payoff. In Mali, organic fair trade seed cotton was purchased from producers at CFA F304/ kg during the 2004/05 season. This price included a biological bonus of CFA F33/kg and a social bonus of CFA F33/kg disbursed to the cooperative. In Burkina Faso, where Helvetas supports a certified organic cotton program, the purchasing price to producers was around 252 CFA F/kg for the 2004/05 season. In Mali, 700 producers participated in organic fair trade cotton production during the 2004/05 season. More than 2,000 are expected for the next season. In Burkina Faso, the Helvetas program reached 72 producers in 2003/04 and 818 in 2005/06. The objective is to have 2,000 organic cotton producers in 2007/08, with a yield of around one ton per hectare.

Producers are selected for the program based on cultivation criteria having to do with the condition of the soil and the presence of organic matter. In order to be certified organic and fair trade, land has to have been fallow for more than three years.

The main obstacles to the development of these niche markets have to do with the current scope of opportunities, the cost of production supervision and the absence of a local textile industry. In the case of the Helvetas program in Mali, seed cotton produced under certified conditions is ginned by Faso Coton (the Swiss trader Reinhart is its main investor) and processed by partners located in India, since there is no local industry capable of making the final product according to certification specifications. In Burkina Faso, fiber cotton is milled locally by Filsah. In any case, the supervision level required to produce organic cotton efficiently is high.

When yields matters and farmers can switch to the production of other cash crops (if they are not satisfied with the returns they are getting from cotton production), the effects of stagnating yields on global efficiency and welfare are muted. Yield stagnation can make cotton production unattractive to farmers in places where other cash crops are an option. During the nineties, stagnating yields in many countries of Central America, as well as in several provinces of China, gave farmers an incentive to switch from cotton production to rice growing (Micarelli 1991). In countries such as Burkina Faso and Mali, farmers have few if any choices for diversification because of several constraints in the short-run. Stagnating yield does not compel WCA farmers to quit cotton production so much as worsen their situation and prospects. Thus, it is crucial to find ways to restore the upward trend in yields in these countries.

What Explains Stagnating Seed Cotton Yields in WCA?

Yield stagnation may be attributable to climatic constraints, which the Cotton-4 cannot influence but should adjust to.[2] Indeed, a reduction in rainfall has played a critical role in making cotton production less secure in the Sahel region during the last 20 years. In spite of climatic conditions that negatively affected expected revenues, Sahel farmers kept producing cotton because of limited cash crop opportunities (Fock 1998).

Beyond climate change and other exogenous factors, the most important reasons for stagnating yields have to do with the quality of technical practices and extension services, which in many places resulted in soil nutriment mining and alleged buildups in pests and diseases. The cost of research and extension is generally considered to be part of the global cost of the cotton sector functioning (critical function). At the request of ginners (Burkina Faso, Chad, and Mali) or the sector association (Benin), National Research Institutes come up with technical recommendations, aimed at maximizing—within technical and budget constraints—cotton yields, ginning out-turn ratio and quality. These recommendations are based on tests meant to show the results that the sector could reach in terms of yields, ginning ratio and quality through a given variety of seeds, set of inputs (fertilizers, herbicides, pesticides) and equipment (the so-called "technical package"). Recommendations are disseminated through extension services, which strive to transmit know-how to producers in an effective manner. Poorly designed or implemented technical practices may negatively affect yields.

Stagnating yields may be the result of producers having little incentive to implement technical recommendations. Indeed, from a producer perspective, yield is a means of maximizing revenue but it is not an end in itself. As emphasized by Fock (1998), increasing yields does not always lead to higher revenues for producers. Beyond certain levels, increasing yields may result in a reduction in income for the producer[3]. Critical levels are determined by the trend and volatility of input prices and seed cotton prices. Risks, which may affect these prices, need to be carefully monitored. Beyond macro shocks, these risks may take various forms, such as delays in the collection of the seed cotton and the payment of producer prices, and disruptions to the timely availability of different components of the technical package (seeds, fertilizers, pesticides, herbicides, and equipment), etc. When these risks happen and the gap between expected seed cotton prices and expected input prices shrinks, it might not be rational for farmers to follow the technical recommendations. In other words, from the producers' point of view, the technical optimum may not match the economic optimum. Bridging the gap between the two optima requires aligning incentives with objectives.

Within the Cotton-4, the approach used to fund research and extension has varied, and this has been reflected in different performance outcomes. In countries such as Benin,

---

2. Some preventive measures may be taken though.

3. Producers' returns are not linear. Indeed, producers may be motivated to enter the cotton market not only by the earnings but also by the opportunity for access to credit and cotton inputs, some of which they can deviate to cereal production and thereby be food-sufficient. Belonging to the cotton club also gives access to valuable extension services. Regardless of the volume of seed cotton they produce, peasant families can also have access to a number of shared facilities, such as schools. In conclusion, producers' returns decrease when their production rises.

research and extension is referred to as a semi-public good, the cost of which is supposed to be borne by both the State and the private sector. However, the conditions for this partnership were not clarified before the private sector came in. As a result, the good has been provisioned insufficiently. Donors have tried to compensate the lack of funding through direct support to AIC. Sustainability is doubtful. In Mali and Burkina Faso, research and extension are considered specific assets, which must be paid by the ginner(s). As a result, only ginners with a relatively large financial capacity and an easy access to best available know-how have been targeted in the process of privatization. In Burkina Faso, where the privatization process is well advanced, the private sector has provided adequate funding for research and extension.

How Can Technical Practices in WCA be Improved?

Technical practices can be improved by strengthening research and extension to enhance on-farm application efficiency and / or by improving input distribution systems to reduce input costs. Both options are considered hereinafter.

Strengthen Research and Extension

Enhancing the competitiveness of the Cotton-4 would require to improve both research and extension services. Strengthening research can help ensuring that improved technologies are generated. Strengthening extension can help ensuring that the improved technologies are transferred effectively to farmers. It is important to use both means to enhance on-farm application efficiency.

Update Fertilizer Formulas. Technical packages currently used in WCA are based on in-depth soil analysis done between 1965 and 1970 by the Cotton and Textile Research Institute (IRCT). These analyses were performed after a series of studies on fertilizer doses meant at improving technical recommendations on the fertilization of cotton trees (see Box 3). Fertilizer formulas were developed on the basis of these studies and have barely changed since.

The fact that fertilizer formulas have not changed in thirty-five years is particularly surprising given that soil and climate conditions have changed since then. Two reasons may explain the lack of up-to-date research.

(a) *First, formulas are tested in the station and not in the fields, where the efficiency of a given package would certainly be lower.* What simple plant analyses show in the field is not necessarily obvious or even visible in the station. Yet, technical updates are not done on the basis of on-farm trials, and it takes a lot of time and funding to implement large-scale soil analysis.

(b) *Secondly, cotton companies allocate limited financial resources to research. This is even more likely to be the case if the sector was privatized without clearly defining which party is responsible for research and extension.* In WCA, privatization often took place without determining whether research and extension was to be a private or public good. Some supported the idea that research and extension is a private good,

---

Box 3: Origins of the Fertilizer Formulas Used in the Cotton-4

During the 1960s, IRCT launched a series of analyses structured around three components: 1) A study of mineral deficiencies using the (N, P, K, S) method; 2) A study of mineral equilibrium with N, P, K as the main elements, using the method developed by L. Richard and 3) Multi-locality tests of fertilizer formula.

The main conclusions, regarding the tropical ferruginous soils covering most of the cotton zones, revealed widespread deficits in phosphorus (P), occasional need of potassium (K), strong need of nitrogen (N) and relatively low need of sulfur (S), except for during land clearing and when fallow lands were being re-cultivated. In regions down south with weak ferruginous soils (such as earth bar of south Benin and Togo), deficits were very similar except in two elements. A lack of phosphorus was less common whereas a lack of potassium was more common and widespread. Research recommendations were based on these conclusions and adapted to constraints based upon industrial feasibility. In the end, a 14-23-14-5-1 formula was largely adopted. The 200 kg/ha dosage considered too high and costly for the farmer, it was lowered to 150 kg/ha. Research recommendations that suggested using a formula different from those suited to tropical ferruginous soils on Benin's poorly ferruginous were ignored. A decision was taken to recommend 100 kg/ha of a 14-23-14 formula, complemented by 50 kg/ha of KC1.

According to the work done by the International Fertilizer Development Center (IFDC) within the context of its Regional Input Market (MIR) project, the formula did not change a bit in Burkina Faso (14-23-14-5-1 formula, with a dosage at 150 kg/ha and a supplement in urea). In Mali, patterns are somewhat diversified, depending on the region and type of farming. In equipped farms, the use of organic fertilizer (manure) has made it possible to reduce the dose of chemical formulas (from 150 kg/ha to 100 kg/ha on average, for any type of formula). In Bougouni and Kita regions, the formula used (14-22-1 2-6-1 formula, with a dosage at 150 kg/ha and a supplement in urea) remains very close to the recommendations made by IRCT thirty-five years ago. Some progress has been observed in the old cotton basin, using a formula enriched in potassium (14-18-18-6-1 formula, with a dosage at150 kg/ha and a supplement in urea). For poorly ferruginous soils and for the tropical ferruginous soils of Benin, the fertilizer formula has remained the same (14-23-14-5-1 formula). The dose is 150 kg/ha for tropical ferruginous soils, to which a urea supplement is added. For poorly ferruginous soils, the dose is 100 kg/ha, but no potassium enrichment takes place despite significant needs.

Source: Gaborel and Houngnibo 2005.

and therefore needs to be paid for by the incoming investors, while other favored the idea that it is a public (or a semi-public) good, which must be funded through (at least partially) the State budget. In some countries, Benin for instance, privatization was structured in such a way as to imply that the good is semi-public and its cost should not be entirely borne by potential investors. In other countries, such as Burkina Faso, the cost of research and extension services was simply deemed part of the cost of doing business in the cotton sector, and only investors with pockets deep enough to cover this cost have the possibility of entering the market. This view acknowledges that research and extension services involve investing in specific assets, which only vertical arrangements can secure.[4] At any rate, research and extension is a critical link in the cotton supply chain, and it is, therefore, crucial to have a common understanding of whose obligation it is (semi-public good or not) prior to privatization so that the right procurement incentives are put into place.

---

4. In theory, research and extension services can be provided through contracting or integration.

According to Gaborel and Houngnibo (2005), nitrogen-enriched formulas would be more effective than the current formulas, but extension services would need to be significantly strengthened to ensure their efficient use. Currently, only northern Cameroon uses unique formulas, which are nitrogen-enriched. This fertilizer approach may not appeal to farmers indeed, as it is specific to cotton and enable no diversion to the fertilization of food crops. However, these unique formulas are of great interest to strengthen yields. Moreover, they are likely to be the most adequate fertilizer approach in low rainfall and short season zones.

Improve Seed Variety. Worldwide the latest improvement in seed variety has been made through the introduction of Genetically Modified (GM) cotton. So far, GM research has been essentially focused on the possible development of the BT gene (*Bacillus thuringiensis* is a naturally occurring soil bacterium used as a biological pesticide—see Box 4 on the economics of GMO). In WCA, gene research geared to developing herbicide resistant cotton would perhaps be most useful as farms are poorly equipped.

In Burkina Faso, significant research has been conducted to screen cotton varieties developed in other countries with the BT gene and see how well they perform in Burkina Faso's growing environment. After three rounds of tests in the station, efficiency studies suggest that the BT gene could significantly improve the cotton chain's performance in Burkina Faso. According to preliminary results, introduction of the BT gene into cotton could help reduce insecticide costs. Although research recommends six insecticide sprayings for each season of traditional seeds, only one or two would be required with BT cotton. Another potential source of savings is the increase in yield. According to station tests done on a variety of samples, yields could be increased by 15 to 35 percent without affecting fiber quality (length, resistance and whiteness). Results on possible costs saving and yield improvement remain controversial. Moreover, one of the risks associated with BT crops is that insects exposed with to BT crops could develop resistance to the BT toxin, which would render conventional (spray) pesticides ineffective.

The creation of a local variety of the new seed containing the BT gene (Monsanto's property) is scheduled for 2007/08. Tests would need to be performed on this new variety to provide a fuller understanding of the effects of introducing the BT gene into cotton production in Burkina Faso. This upcoming transgenic variety might have very different properties than the varieties tested so far. The reduction in insecticide sprayings from six to one or two—without affecting yield or fiber quality—remains to be confirmed with tests in the station and in the field. Similarly, work needs to be done to better understand the impact of BT cotton on health and the environment, as well as effects down the road on cotton-based industries and manufacturing.

Several issues must be dealt with before introducing a local variety of cotton with the BT gene, such as defining a regulatory framework and clarifying the property rights of the newly created seed. In Burkina Faso, most stakeholders in the cotton chain tend to think that the sector's future success depends upon adopting GM cotton, and the government has just passed a law to provide them with a sound regulatory framework. In countries such as Mali, opinions are mixed and it is wise to give stakeholders in the cotton chain an opportunity to reflect on the pros and cons of adopting (or not) this technology. In Benin, a moratorium has been imposed that prevents any action on the issue at this time. To facilitate upcoming efforts, the World Bank is performing a project meant at improving bio-safety through a strengthened bio-safety framework. The objective also is to build

---

Box 4: The Economics of Genetically Modified Cotton

Genetically modified (GM) cotton, a result of technological developments in the 1990s, has the potential to reduce the cost of production and hence increase profitability among early adopters of this technology. In effect, GM-type cotton (as well as all other GM products) acts as insurance against pests, insects, or weeds. The grower pays a premium for the pest-resistant seed (as they would when buying other types of insurance). If an insect attacks the crop, the grower's benefit comes through the lower costs of not spraying. For example, the average number of pesticide applications used against bollworms in the United States fell from 4.6 in 1992–1995 to 0.8 in 1999–2001. Furthermore, the grower is likely to experience higher yields because spraying conventional cotton usually reduces yields. For example, yield increases due to switching to GM cotton range from 19 percent (China) to 80 percent (India). In developing countries there may also be health benefits because small growers spray with hand-held devises and, thus, any reduction in spraying would also imply a reduced risk of poisoning. On the other hand, if the insect does not attack the crop, growers simply lose their premium (i.e. the cost difference between conventional and GM cotton). Research has shown that, on balance, GM cotton users are much better off compared to users of conventional cotton.

There are two types of GM cotton: Bt cotton and herbicide-tolerant cotton. *Bt (Bacillus thuringiensis)* is a naturally occurring soil bacterium that has been used as a biological pesticide for many years. The gene that produces the relevant insect toxin has been transferred from that bacterium into the cotton plant, which means that the plant is capable of producing its own toxin and the grower, therefore, does not need to apply pesticides. Herbicide-tolerant cotton is a cotton plant that has been genetically modified to resist herbicides that would otherwise kill both weeds and the cotton plant. Consequently, the herbicide can be applied without exterminating the cotton plant.

Producing GM cotton is a multi-step and complicated process, which is the reason most developing cotton-producing countries have not embraced the technology. First, the legal and regulatory framework must be established to address issues such as the selection of the company to undertake trials, pricing, the copyright of genetic material, whether growers are allowed to recycle GM seeds or must purchase the seeds every year, time-duration of the GM license, etc. The second stage involves field trials to develop seeds appropriate to local growing conditions. For example, there are about 35 GM cotton varieties in the United States and 22 in China, each designed for particular pest populations and growing conditions. The third stage involves actual adaptation by the cotton growers.

Who receives the benefits of GM cotton? There are four groups whose welfare is likely to be affected by the use of GM seeds: the companies that manufacture the seeds, the farmers that use them, the farmers that do not use them, and the consumers. Falk-Zepeda et al. (2000) estimated that of the $215 million in surplus generated in 1996–1998 per year due to the switch from conventional to GM cotton varieties in the United States, U.S. farmers' net income increased by $105 million while the seed companies received $80 million. Increased cotton output reduced world prices, generating about $45 million in consumer savings (both in the United States and elsewhere), but cotton farmers in other countries (i.e., farmers that did not use GM cotton) lost an estimated $15 million because of lower cotton prices. The methodology of these welfare effects was based on a standard economic surplus model developed by Alston et al. (1995).

Source: FAO (2004), pp. 41–57.

bio-safety capacity that permits a holistic evaluation of transgenic crops, consistent with the implementation of the Cartagena Protocol on Bio-safety while seizing the opportunity for the establishment of research and regulatory framework in West Africa.

Further Develop Integrated Management Programs. It is getting more and more critical to adopt integrated management programs, which allow improvements to fertilizer efficiency while reducing soil washout, nutrient loss, and environmental risks. The objective is to facilitate a better integration of mineral fertilizers and organic resources to strengthen the efficiency of mineral fertilizers, improve organic matter, and reduce environmental risks. Integrated management is based on better usage of soil nutrients, locally available amendments (for example, harvest residues, compost, manure) and mineral fertilizers to improve productivity.

Improved cultivation techniques are most likely to be achieved through strengthened extension services and a better use of mineral and organic fertilizers.

Intensifying production means not only increasing the quantity and quality of mineral and organic fertilizers but also improving cultivation practices and technical monitoring. Efficient use of water is often an important component of integrated management. Furthermore, work has been done that shows the significance of better fertilizer usage (timing of use, duration of use, dosage). Farmers must also be better trained and become more involved in managing their soils.

Intensification of production and subsequent increases in yields can only come through the combined utilization of mineral and organic fertilizers. The role of organic fertilizers is crucial in soil preparation since they improve the efficiency of mineral fertilizers.

However, organic matter cannot serve as a substitute for mineral fertilizers. Indeed, organic manure has poor nutrient content and is not always available in sufficient quantities. Moreover, extending the use of organic manure implies increasing livestock production in regions where pressure on land is already great and exacerbating tensions between producers and herders.[5] Further research is needed to reopen discussion on agriculture/livestock competition, taking into account new challenges and assessments.

Nevertheless, assuming that tensions between producers and herders can be kept under control, yields can increase substantially if organic manure and additional equipment were introduced. In Burkina Faso, yield could increase from around 700 Kg/ha to a national average of 1,000 Kg/ha (all plantings included). Gross revenue would go from 122,500 CFA F (700 Kg * 1 ha * 175 CFA F/Kg) to 1,050,000 CFA F (1,200 Kg * 5 ha * 175 CFA F/Kg). The farmer that cultivates with difficulties and very inefficiently 1 hectare of cotton and 1 hectare of cereals (food needs) with his "daba," or hoe, could cultivate 5 hectares of cotton and 2 hectares of cereals if he were equipped with a pair of oxen, "multiculteurs" or other types of toolbars, a seed drill and a cart. In terms of cotton production, the availability of these tools would allow him to do his work at the right moment (plowing and seed during first rainfall, hoeing when the field is covered with weeds, etc.).

Cotton chain stakeholders are aware of this, but are facing high equipment costs and problems getting credit to purchase that equipment (see Table 4). In fact, only those farmers who are equipped with a pair of oxen, multiculteur-type toolbars, seed drill and a cart can use organic manure. In Burkina Faso, only 60 percent of farms have these basic equipments. It is generally difficult for farmers to get a loan to buy such equipments as there is only one bank, with limited capacity, which is specialized in agriculture financing.

---

5. Some possible solutions might include allowing forage crops alongside cotton crops (as a cheap way of feeding livestock), looking at land ownership, and having field and tree-park enclosures at lot level. The most remarkable new development is that the majority of livestock in the cotton zones of Mali and Burkina Faso now belong to farmers rather than to traditional pastoralists or nomadic herders, as was the case 15 years ago.

Table 4. Cost of Equipment in Burkina Faso, 2005/06

	Cost '000 CFA F	Comments
Pair of oxen	250	would be the contribution of the producer (33%)
Multiculteur toolbars	150	plow, butteur, hoeing
seed drill	110	cotton, maize
Cart	240	Organic manure's transport. Traction by donkey extra
Total	750	

Source: SOFITEX, 2005.

The cost of credit is rather high (around 15 percent) as risks associated with this sort of lending are high and the lending capacity is low.

Encourage Best Use of Herbicides. Herbicide usage is the easiest means for a farmer to increase the area under cultivation and thereby maintain his total revenue when seed cotton prices drop. Herbicides allow farmers, who have limited workforce and equipment, to control weed growth over greater expanses of land. Increasing the area of cultivated land has had an effect not only the efficiency of cotton production, but on the global performance of farming. Herbicides, too, have played a critical role in this trend.

However, in order to improve herbicide usage, it is necessary to determine which strategy offers the farmer the highest payoff: more cultivated land with more herbicide use, or better cultivation practices aimed at greater efficiency. If amplifying the surface area under cultivation (necessitating greater use of herbicides) does not earn the farmer more than what he could get by adhering more closely to the technical recommendations, yet he pursues this strategy (which has negative effects on the land that his livelihood depends on) anyway, then perhaps the farmer would benefit from additional explanation and supervision. Otherwise, alternative solutions need to be found, including, in extreme cases, explicit measures to limit cultivated areas. Currently, farmers request inputs—particularly herbicides—without paying any heed to technical recommendations. They seem to prefer having an excess supply so that they do not have to apply it sparingly or will have enough left over for use on other crops. This year in Mali, herbicide requests were nearly double the amount prescribed in technical recommendations, amounting to 180 percent.

Reduce Input Costs

Much effort has been expended over many years to identify ways of reducing input costs, which consume about one third of producers' gross-revenues in WCA. IFDC (2005), a main contributor to this global effort, estimates that farmers could save 20 to 30 percent of what they pay to get fertilizers. In particular, it show that input costs could be diminished most notably by improving procurement, professionalizing input transport and distribution, and harmonizing regional import rules.

Improve Input Price Setting. In WCA there is generally a single countrywide price for fertilizers and a single countrywide price for insecticides, irrespective of the particular

Table 5. Input Costs in 2004/05 (CFA Francs)

	Seed	Fertilizer NPKSB	Urea Fertilizer	Herbicide	Insecticides	Treatment equipment	Packaging cost
	2 bags of 30 kg	bag of 50 kg	bag of 50 kg	Per liter		1 for 3 years	
Benin		10,250	10,250		3,900/flacon		
Burkina Faso[6]	1800	13,500	13,500	5,311	4,867/litre	25,995	107,122
Cote d'Ivoire		13,000	12,000		4,500/litre		
Mali		14,700	14,200		4,770/litre		
Togo		13,200	13,200		4,800/litre		

Source: ICA, SOFITEX, CMDT, 2005.

formulation For example Table 5 shows that in general the price for fertilizer is the same if the fertilizer is urea or NPKSB. The official explanation is that farmers are uneducated and have very little comprehension of the effects of different fertilizers. If they were able to select between fertilizers and purchase at the real price they would use excessive amounts of urea to the detriment of the cotton crop. This is hardly consistent with the observed capacity of even subsistence farmers elsewhere (see PADECO 2006).

Current setting of input prices offers the possibility for input suppliers to profit from supply of the cheaper urea when farmers require the more expensive NPKB. The situation with insecticide can result in even more serious problems when totally inappropriate insecticides are applied.

Improve the Effectiveness of Procurement. Inputs are supplied by national or international providers, which satisfy the terms of tenders that are organized annually. The terms of the tenders specify the types of input needed and the characteristic of the companies sought to supply the market. All input procurements enjoy a supplier credit covering all needs. The granting of credits is a condition spelt out in the terms of the tenders for a period of over 200 days (for example, 240 days in Mali, 270 days in Burkina Faso).

Very few suppliers have actually the capacity and the incentives for granting the credits required by the terms of the tenders. The length of credit required by the terms of the tenders is long and ginners can go bankrupt over extended periods. As a result, the cost for providing such credits is high. Suppliers with the financial capacity needed to grant these credits may want to serve less risky buyers. Thus, only fertilizer suppliers who are risk takers and have pockets deep enough might be willing to be in the market. Moreover, markets for fertilizer in WCA are relatively small, further narrowing the number of credible bidders.

---

6. If technical recommendations are followed, respective share of input costs are the following: seed (2 percent), fertilizer (36 percent), urea (12 percent), herbicide (15 percent), insecticides (27 percent), treatment equipment (8 percent).

Hence, the system of fertilizer procurement may put suppliers in a dominant position[7] throughout the different markets of the subregion and with dominant players come all types of risks of abuse of dominant position. Given that fertilizer purchases take place more or less at the same time throughout the subregion, the risk of suppliers abusing their dominant position is actually great. If a particular supplier is selected by several countries at the same time and does not have the capacity to honor all his purchase agreements, then he may seek to collude with other potential suppliers so that together they can control the markets of the region.[8]

The procurement method used for fertilizer purchases is particularly problematic because legislation on competition is rarely enforced in WCA. The National Commission on Competition and Consumption in Burkina Faso, for example, states in its progress report that legislation governing this area is not enforced for the most part. The absence of litigation, not only civil or administrative, but also criminal largely confirms this. According to this Commission,

> However, infringements are numerous and cause serious prejudice to businesses. Very often, these infringements are communicated to administrative authorities or through the media or economic operators, but administrative authorities rarely react, and never in the sense of repression (NCCC 2000:16).

In this same report, it is noted that calls for tenders are often used to prevent competition: "Call for tenders' market sector seems to be the preferred ground for practices against competition, namely collusion on prices and market sharing" (NCCC 2000).

Of course, this statement does not imply that the call for tenders is an inappropriate method for procuring inputs. What it suggests, instead, is that different procurement methods yield different results, depending on circumstances. A call for tenders is very effective when potential suppliers are diverse and numerous. It is very ineffective when there are few potential suppliers. Conversely, sole sourcing is highly inappropriate when the number of potential suppliers is large but might be a relevant approach to procurement when there are very few suppliers who meet the technical specifications.

Regional calls for tenders are not a solution. The market for fertilizers remains too small, even on a regional level, to attract a large enough number of suppliers. Thus, a regional call for tender is a poor method of procurement for WCA. What is worse, regionalizing procurement could open the door to greater collusion and corruption.

One reform would involve changing the calendar for fertilizer purchases. More thought needs to be given to better designing calls for tenders so that the buyers can benefit from the seasonality of fertilizer prices. Indeed, fertilizer prices vary up to 30 percent in the course of the year. Currently, in WCA, fertilizers are customarily purchased during the peak season (in autumn), when they should be purchased off-peak. As is the case for most

---

7. Antitrust laws define dominant position and the potential issue of abuse of a dominant position relatively to the 30% of the market-share threshold.

8. Regional procurement of fertilizers, as is sometimes proposed, does not seem to address the problem. Indeed, if fertilizers were procured regionally instead of nationally, corruption would likely expand. Moreover, if regional procurement were organized, local factories could not supply all countries at the same time and an upward price trend would likely occur (local capacity is estimated at 750,000 tons as compared with the 1.2 million tons used).

Table 6. Statistical and Tariff Nomenclature of the WAEMU

Category	Customs	Statistical tax	Communauty duty
0	0%	1%	1%
1	5%	1%	1%
2	10%	1%	1%
3	20%	1%	1%

Source: WAEMU, 2005.

oil products, fertilizer prices reflect a strong seasonality, which should be exploited to allow better management of purchases. Of course, changing the calendar for fertilizer purchases would have an impact on storage costs and purchasing when prices are low will not reduce costs of the fertilizers if the extra cost for storage exceeds the saving made. While further analysis would be needed to establish thresholds, it is very unlikely that the extra-cost for storage would surpass savings, which could come from improved purchases of fertilizers.

Better management of the purchase calendar should become a priority but it must be matched by improvements to village storage facilities. The ideal situation is to have sufficient infrastructure so as to be able to purchase fertilizers at the best moment (when prices are lowest) and store them under appropriate conditions at the village level. Burkina Faso's National Union of Cotton Producers has come up with a proposal along these lines, known by the slogan: "One Union of Cotton Producers—One Shop." The objective is to warehouse the various inputs, under proper conditions, before distributing them to users at the right moment. In cases where fertilizers are not used, the existence of storage facilities would allow better assessment of what is in stock and discounts to the GPC (Groupement de Producteurs de Coton). It should be noted that the Action Plan for the Implementation of a Strategic Development Framework of the cotton chain in Burkina Faso[9] already includes building infrastructure in villages.

Harmonizing Regional Importation Rules to Reduce Pesticide Costs. To make pesticide use easier for farmers, research recommends using pre-mixed pesticides, imported in end-user packaging (half liter bottles). Yet, the statistical and tariff nomenclature of the WAEMU has a different taxation system for insecticides based on whether they are sold in end-user packaging or in other forms of packaging. Indeed, according to section VI, chapter 38 of this nomenclature, packaged pesticides for retail are classified under the code 38.08.10.10.00 that follows a third category taxation (see Table 6 above) whereas other packaged pesticides are classified under the code 38.08.10.90.00, which follows a first category taxation.

---

9. A shop costs around CFA F 7 million; in Burkina, about 9,000 GPCs are operational. Priority needs in village infrastructure have been identified by UNPCB, which estimates that 261 shops should be built at a cost of 1,821 billion CFA F.

Revising the statistical and tariff nomenclature of WAEMU, so that insecticides imported in end-user packaging are taxed the same as other insecticides, would reduce the cost of pesticides to producers. Given that insecticide costs represent more than 25 percent of the farmer's technical package, this change would be very significant in terms of potential savings. In Burkina Faso, for example, the savings would be on the order of CFA F 2 billion. Of course, the government subsidy for inputs would have to be reduced by the same amount, which would simplify input financing.

An alternative solution would entail importing pure, non-diluted products, rather than mixes, and having the mixing process done by local industries, or even farmers. However, these solutions are not without costs. The first solution implies the existence of a mixing factory with sufficient capacity, both in terms of volume and quality control. The second solution would require significant strengthening of extension services to farmers.

Improving Input Distribution. Input distribution could be enhanced by rationalizing transportation, facilitating trade, and reducing the markup of local distributors. Interregional transportation costs (including border-crossing and roadblocks costs) account for one fifth of the price producers in countries such as Mali pay for fertilizer. These costs are 1.5 times more expensive than maritime transportation costs. If interregional transportation costs were cut in half, it would be possible for the Malian cotton producer to save more than 25 CFA F/T.[10] The most obvious way to reduce transportation costs is through rationalization. In Mali, for instance, 70 percent of the trucks carrying fertilizer into the country return to the coast empty, when they could be used to transport cotton lint (as is the case in Burkina Faso, for instance). Input distribution is another key problem for the cotton sector in WCA, as local distributors charge a relatively high price (markup is approximately 10 percent of Cost, Assurance and Freight or CAF price in Bamako) for their services. Professionalizing distribution could significantly improve input costs.

---

10. This example derives from IFDC (2005) for urea.

CHAPTER 3

Reducing Post-harvest Costs and Improving Quality

Ilhem Baghdadli and Gael Raballand

Diagnosing costs and the influence of reliable grading on sales revenues are prerequisites to reducing costs and improving grading. The task is tricky because the cost structure of ginners varies among the Cotton-4; if there are several ginners in a country (as is the case in Benin and Burkina Faso), it also varies from one ginner to another. Differences in production costs are reported to be significant. They are caused by a variety of factors, such as past and current strategies. Of course, market structure and organization also have a huge impact on market performance. Given that cost structures are significantly different from one Cotton-4 country to another, there is necessarily room for improvement; and because cost structures are literally inherited, improving the cost structure of cotton companies has to be done on a case-by-case basis. Moreover, a strategy aimed at reducing costs must be global and must take into account how best to manage risks along the chain. The goal is not to minimize each cost component but rather the total costs along the supply chain. Indeed, decreasing the cost of doing an activity along the supply chain may result in transferring risks to vertically related activities, eventually increasing the cost of doing other activities along the chain. For instance, decreasing the cost of transport by outsourcing it to the lowest bidder could end up increasing the cost of storage for both producers and ginners (at either the ginning factory or the port), as well as increasing the risk that contracts are not carried out on time.

Lessons learned from international and multi-sector best practices suggest it is crucial to understand how the various cost components of the cotton supply chain relate to one another—their interdependency—and the risks involved in making changes to any one component. For a ginner, for instance, outsourcing transport to a third-party carries free-riding risks, which might be hard to tackle when transport services alter input supplies, seed cotton collection and lint-cotton deliveries. The reliability of grading is another risk that can jeopardize WCA cotton supply chains, which are small players competing with a large array of quality producers. As for seed cotton pricing schemes, they do more than establish how to split risks between the ginner and the producers. They also determine the level of risk that the sector will have to bear, regardless, and the contingent liability that the government (implicitly) agrees to support. All in all, minimizing costs and improving grading implies managing risks, and what this section aims to illuminate is that market structure and organization are natural tools for managing risks.

What are the Main Costs and Risks Borne by Ginners?

Cotton companies in WCA have no obligation or incentive to reveal their cost structure. Cotton companies in the region are not listed on the stock market, and they are owned by a limited number of investors, who have no obligation to release their financial information to the public. If the companies decided, however, to disclose their costs, this would weaken their bargaining power with traders or textile merchants, who represent the driving force behind the market for cotton. Secondly, such a decision would weaken the companies' ability to get support from their governments when international market prices fall. For several decades, cotton has been a major source of growth in Benin, Burkina Faso, Chad, and Mali. When the cotton sector experiences severe shocks, governments try to keep it from "snowballing"—affecting other sectors and sending the economy as a whole into a downward spiral. Experience shows, however, that it is difficult to keep the risk of contingent liabilities at the lowest possible level without distorting firms' behavior. Given that they receive support when facing difficulties, cotton companies have nothing to gain by saying that they are doing well. In fact, the opposite is true.

Thus, public information on the cost structures of the cotton companies in WCA consists of data that may be deliberately overestimated. Publicly available data suggest, however, that the main cost components are: the price of seed cotton, the price of inputs, transport and ginning. Overhead costs sometimes reportedly exceed the cost of providing research and extension (4 percent versus 3 percent, according to Gergely 2004). Cost certification is needed to go beyond rough average figures.

Enhancing the cost structure of the cotton companies in WCA would require a tailored approach to best manage the main components of the companies' cost structures and identify the arrangements needed to minimize risks along the cotton supply chain. Indeed, decreasing the cost of doing an activity along the supply chain may result in transferring risks to vertically related activities, eventually increasing the cost of doing other activities along the chain. Transport, grading and seed cotton pricing rules are among the most critical vehicles for risks.

Outsourcing transport to a third-party carries free-riding risks, as timely and quality transport services are vital when it comes to input supplies, seed cotton collection and cotton lint deliveries. If inputs are not provided on time, the whole process of production may be dramatically altered. Problems may also ensue if seed cotton is not collected on time, as it may rain while the seed cotton is still stored in the open air. The timing of lint-cotton deliveries is a very important condition of any sales contract. If the timing is not respected, the contract can be void, possibly resulting in significant penalties.

The reliability of grading is another risk, which may jeopardize WCA cotton supply chains. Major defects due to contamination of the lint cotton are imperceptible until the lint is processed by the textile industry and it breaks. Given the speed with which the textile industry operates, it is already too late for the end-buyer, who as a result of contamination early on in the supply chain will be unable to honor the contracts he has with his clients in the clothing industry. Since the price of lint cotton represents a very small portion of the costs incurred in making fabric, buying cotton from risky origins makes no sense when there is so much available worldwide. Achieving reliable grading is a goal that demands committed and continuous effort, and the benefits that accrue from it can vanish with just one year of unreliable grading.

Another major risk is shaped when deciding on seed cotton pricing schemes. Indeed, pricing schemes are agreements, which do more than establish the division of risk between the ginner and the producers. These pricing schemes also determine the level of risk that the entire sector will have to bear, and can have a negative impact, down the road, on the profits that producers and ginners share.

What is the Way to Minimize Risk When Designing Seed Cotton Pricing Schemes?

Why Two-tier Prices?

In WCA, the price of seed cotton has traditionally been broken into two payments as producers are absolutely risk-averse, and the length of any given season brings considerable risks of intra-seasonal volatility. An initial price is announced before planting and paid during the season (see Box 1 in Chapter 1). If the marketing season is good and there are profits to distribute, a bonus can be paid to producers at the end of the season. If the marketing season is bad, there is nothing to distribute. In the worst-case scenario, revenues earned during the season are less than the commitment made when the initial price was announced. In this case, ginners (and /or producers) may want to use monies from a stabilization fund they may have set up to complete payment based on the initial price.

The Risks at Stake for Farmers and Ginners. There are costs to moving from a two-tier price to a one-tier price (whether paid before the season begins or after it has ended). Changing the pricing scheme for seed cotton implies changing the level of risk borne within the sector and the way risks are shared between partners. If seed cotton were paid for just once, before planting, producers would bear less risk than they do now with a two-tier payment. Conversely, ginners would bear more risk and they would charge producers for that. The other extreme would entail paying for seed cotton once the marketing campaign is over. Producers, however, don't have the liquidity to cover all the expenses they have to bear during the season, and even if they could offer to do this, and wanted to, they may not trust the company to compensate them fairly for this service.

There are different types of two-tier pricing-schemes, and each one brings a specific level of risk for ginners and producers. For ginners, risks are:

    (i)   relatively low, if the initial price covers no more than the sunk costs borne by the producers, when planting

    (ii) high, if the setting of the initial price aims to cover all fixed costs borne by the producers, during the season

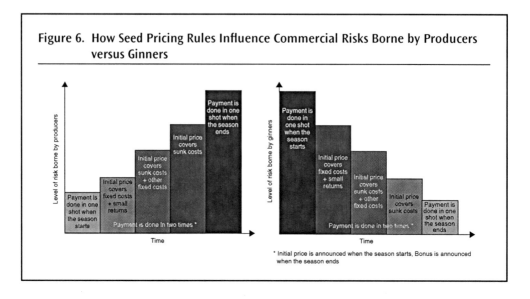

Figure 6. How Seed Pricing Rules Influence Commercial Risks Borne by Producers versus Ginners

(iii) highest, if the initial price is meant to be set above costs. Indeed, committing a year ahead to pay for returns, which simply may not materialize, has dramatic effects on a ginner's ability to cope with potential risks.

Risks patterns are the reverse for producers.

Achieving Competitiveness Among Different Types of Producers. There are a variety of producers, having different cultivated area, equipment, knowledge and credit. Yet, these differing capacities result in different levels of cost effectiveness. The farmers who are best equipped and have the largest cultivated area are much more efficient than farmers who have a small cultivated area and no equipment, for instance.

Given that there is no such thing as an average cotton producer, setting price at cost raises important issues. First it must be decided whose costs are being used: the costs of the best performers, the costs of the worst performers or those of some sort of average performer. Setting initial prices to provide incentives for the worst performers, would certainly lead to the greatest tonnage of production at the highest cost. Conversely, if the initial price is set so as to cover the costs of the best performer, the least efficient producers may be unable to produce cotton. Governments often argue that these producers are actually the poorest and that it is mandatory to set seed cotton prices in a way that will enable them to be among cotton's beneficiaries. On the other hand, the very principle of shared growth assumes that the conditions enabling growth are met. If they are not, there will be nothing to share with the poorest. Moreover, when the level of initial prices is exaggerated, ginners have less incentive to perform well and thereby enhance market efficiency and welfare.

The setting of an initial price "selects" who is in and who is out of seed cotton production. The higher the price, the larger will be the pool of farmers, for whom cotton production is profitable. When monitoring tools do not enable sorting producers according to their cost-effectiveness, it can be very ineffective to try to set price at costs. Conversely, ginners must: 1) identify what they can afford to pay producers given their cost structure and events affecting the international market; 2) negotiate with producers and other interests at stakes what portion of this upper limit they will actually pay.

This approach requires sound typologies of producers' patterns. Capacities are currently being built in Mali, where a new typology of farmers is being identified by the Institute of Rural Economics, IER and in Burkina Faso where SOFITEX has dedicated some of its budget for this purpose. Establishing these new typologies in the Cotton-4 is very important. No strategy aimed at enhancing the competitiveness of a sector can be designed without a clear understanding of the strength and weaknesses of the patterns of farmers. Moreover, supporting farmers who have no equipment and are cultivating cotton on a small scale will entail very different political choices and investments than strategies aimed at supporting farmers with more equipment and greater growing areas.

In terms of pricing, the two approaches converge when the "targeted farmers" are reasonably efficient. For the sake of simplicity, we will make this assumption in the following subsection.

What are the Options for Setting the Initial Price?

Paying for Sunk Costs. At planting time, a number of expenditures have to be made by producers, who need to get the technical package recommended by research and extension services for producing the best cotton. These recommendations are relevant only to the production of cotton, and producers may incur sunk costs if the assumptions underlying the specifications of the technical package are not met. For instance, if the expected yields that a farmer can ultimately get diminish significantly a couple of months after planting, making cotton production unprofitable for this farmer, he will not be able to switch to another crop without losing money. Fertilizers are cotton-specific, as are pesticides and, to some extent, herbicides. Land preparation is another important sunk cost.

Because farmers do not have pockets deep enough to be willing to assume the risk of paying sunk costs related to sowing, they require ginners to commit to a minimum seed cotton price before sowing. From the producer's point of view, this initial price should be known before sowing and it should cover, at least, the sunk costs he might bear. From the ginner's point of view, initial prices should be set at the lowest possible level.

Paying for All Fixed Costs. In practice, initial prices are set at levels designed to cover the costs of production of most producers. Moreover, as these costs cannot be estimated objectively, producers and ginners are forced to negotiate them, with the outcome largely determined by the relative bargaining power of the two sides. One of the difficulties of estimating the costs of cotton production—a very labor intensive crop—has to do with the hidden or hard-to-quantify costs of employing family members and relations (including children), who often are not paid in cash. Any change in labor costs is likely to have a significant impact on a farmer's revenues and, therefore, farmers are quick to play this card at the bargaining table. On the other hand, ginners in WCA have to deal with the consequences of poor infrastructure and many other constraints that weaken their potential for competitiveness on international markets and make them disinclined to pay much for labor. If farmers have the upper hand in negotiations, as was the case in Mali following a farmer boycott on cotton production in 2000, they will tend to exaggerate the value of labor. Conversely, when production is poorly structured and farmers have little bargaining power (as is the case in Togo, where producers are not even involved in decision-making on seed cotton prices) negotiations will downplay labor's role.

The choice of a seed cotton pricing scheme based on a formula, rather than annual negotiations, decreases the level of risk that the cotton sector has to bear. The outcome of negotiations greatly depends on the relative bargaining power of producers and ginners; as negotiations may be colored by recent events, personal relations and other unpredictable variables, the balance of power can shift from one season to another. This inherent uncertainty affects the market and the perception of risk.

The higher the initial commitment on price, the greater the commercial risk borne by the ginner, which means he may be unable to honor his commitment or pay a bonus. When the initial price aims to cover all of the farmers' costs, and the cost of seed cotton is based on the worst performers, or is simply overestimated, the sector commits to pay for returns that may never materialize. This leads to contingent liabilities for the government and to the sector's bankruptcy if the government cannot pay for these liabilities. The pros and cons of the different seed cotton pricing schemes must therefore be clear to producers and ginners when deciding on a pricing scheme and determining the level of commercial risk they want the sector to pay for. It is also important for governments to prevent having to pay for contingent liabilities by setting rules obliging farmers and ginners to agree on prudent pricing schemes for seed cotton.

What are the Options for Calculating Bonuses?

At the end of the season, ginners know their profit and should be able to draw on it, at no risk, to reward producers for their work with a bonus.

In practice, there is no strict deadline for the closing of a season. Moreover, only ginners know the actual profits of the cotton sector each season. This exclusive information provides ginners with a competitive advantage over producers. Thus producers may not be willing to: 1–wait until the end of the season before they get the second installment of their remuneration, and 2–trust the financial results that the ginner provides.

Thus, sharing actual profits is not always possible, and producers and ginners may agree to share targeted profits. When the asymmetry of information becomes problematic, producers and ginners may agree on using a proxy for calculating profits and a possible bonus. These proxies may involve setting:

    (i) *A predetermined closing date for the season.* For producers, whose savings capacity is small, the sooner the season is closed and they get their bonus, the better. For ginners, who may want to have the flexibility to spread out their sales with the hope of improving their sales revenues, the later the season is closed and they pay producers' bonuses, the better.

    (ii) *Index for sales prices.* As explained in Chapter 4, there are limited options available to approximate sales prices.

    (iii) *Objectives rather than actual costs functions.* In the worst-case scenario, if the company's data cannot be trusted, the parties may want to share gross profits rather than net profits.

When a pricing rule depends on too many proxies, ginners' remuneration can be unrelated to their actual performance. If incentives are lacking, there may be no improvement in the cotton market. A very effective way to avoid the use of proxies is to have producers as shareholders.

Examples

As shown in the examples below, one formula cannot fit all.

Mali. In Mali, the new agreement on seed cotton price (January 2005) is aimed at minimizing the risks borne by the cotton sector and thus maximizing the profits to be shared at the end of the season. A commitment was made to set an initial price prudently— that is, relatively low for producers but enabling them to get a significant share of any profits.

The setting of a relatively low initial price is meant to minimize commercial risks, which might translate into fiscal risk. The Malian producer assumes that the initial price should be set according to the actual breakeven cost of the ginner, which, a year ahead, can only be roughly estimated based on assumptions about internal cotton prices, exchange rates and the retail price for seed. The initial price is said to be prudent because its calculation relies on quite conservative assumptions for world cotton prices (55 cents per pound), exchange rates (US$1 = €1.2) and the retail price for seed (CFA F 44 per kilo). This pricing scheme suggests that the initial price need not cover producers' fixed costs. The underlying idea is that by setting the initial price conservatively, the sector avoids fostering inefficient farmers.

Profit estimates and bonus calculations are derived by using many different proxies:

1. Cotlook A (in annual average) is used to estimate sales prices.
2. Gross profits are shared in a way that is supposed to provide ginners and producers with the revenues they need to soundly cover their costs.
3. The length of the marketing season is predetermined.

As the Malian pricing rule obliges ginners to try and beat the average proxy for international market prices, it may prevent them from selling forward and locking a position, which is perhaps the best way to minimize fiscal risks. That said, ginners must have a good reputation and a lot of credibility to convince producers to be paid on their performance rather than on the average performance of the market. Historically, however, the Malian ginner has had neither a good reputation nor much credibility.

Burkina Faso. The prevailing agreement on seed cotton price in Burkina Faso actually inspired the design of the new Malian seed cotton-pricing rule. It suggests that the initial price is in line with ginners' breakeven cost; and profit estimates and bonus calculations are based on the sector's actual performance (average sale price minus cost) and are paid out during the following season. Compared with the Malian pricing scheme, the advantages of this formula are: (i) it minimizes the level of uncertainty that ginners must bear and thereby the cost they may want to charge (producers) for bearing the risk; and (ii) it smoothes inter-seasonal volatility. Practically, this means that the producers' price is somehow buffered from international markets when prices go down. The disadvantages of the system are: (i) the ginners' sales performances have a direct impact on producers' revenues and this is a problem if the ginner has little or no incentive to perform well; and (ii) the bonus is distributed to farmers a year after cotton production is over. While waiting for the bonus, farmers are retiring from and entering into cotton production. This means that some farmers go un-rewarded for their work while others receive a bonus without having earned it.

What Stabilization Funds Can (and Cannot) Do

Proposals for Regional Stabilization Funds reflect the legacy of the Société Française pour le Développement des Fibres Textiles (CFDT), which in the 1950s established a Stabilization Fund for Cotton Prices in Western Francophone Africa (AOF). Yet, there are several differences between that time and today. Economies are more open, and cotton prices are fixed by world markets.

If the marketing campaign is such that the revenues earned during the season are less than the initial price commitment, monies from a stabilization fund can be used to meet the full payment of the initial price. Stabilization funds rarely satisfy people's high expectations for them, as their endowments are (by nature) limited and they tend to be poorly used.

Price Support Funds, aimed at softening the effect of price shocks, are not meant to prevent these shocks from happening or to remedy the downward trend. In principle, these funds may belong to producers, ginners or the entire cotton sector. They consist of potential donations and are endowed by withholdings on benefits made during profitable years. The funds are to be used during deficit years so that the cotton sector can pay its producers a decent salary and motivate them to continue producing cotton. The objective is two-fold. In the short run, these funds help avoid a possible explosion of the link between fixed costs and variable costs in the event of a dramatic drop in production. The objective in the medium run is to maintain predictable trends in production.

Price Support Funds can only absorb a limited part of the potential effects of price shocks. A Stabilization Fund's potential is limited by its endowment size. Yet, initial endowments allocated to these Funds are limited by the fungibility of donor resources. Meanwhile, withholdings on profits are limited by their size (when they exist at all), and also by the tendency of stakeholders in the sector to want to pocket profits in the present rather than reserve them for a less sunny future.

Experience shows that Price Support Funds can be a source of irrational expectation that substantially distorts market efficiency. In Mali, for example, the Price Support Fund has become the instrument used by the cotton sector to transfer its debts to the government. The results of the 2004/05 season, which were used as the basis for seed cotton price negotiations, were way below predictions. The cotton sector chose to use the Support Fund to cover the deficit, as allowed by the law enforced at that time. The problem is that the Fund was never endowed, and by suggesting the use of such a Fund, the law transformed a contingent liability into an actual debt. Furthermore, the law did not provide the required incentives for cautious management of cotton revenues. On the contrary, the law had become a source of irrational expectation. Mali's previous experience with Support Funds was also a failure. The regulation passed on October 21st, 1999 established principles for managing revenues and risk allocation in the cotton sector. These principles assumed that the fund would be regularly endowed during years of profits. However, when a crisis hit in 2000–01, these funds had disappeared. The cotton company had used them without prior consent from producers to pay for past debts due to poor management. This has totally wrecked producers' confidence and most of them boycotted cotton production the following year, dramatically aggravating the company's management problems.

Even in the best-case scenario, Price Support Funds have produced mixed results. In Burkina Faso, for example, the Support Fund that existed prior to two new ginners entering the market in September 2004, was created by transferring endowments of the previous management facility (a Stabilization Fund). It has not been endowed since then and has been used, with producers' consent, to help finance fertilizer purchases and pay bonuses. Once needs have been identified, direct support with clear utilization clauses may be a better use of funds than earmarking them for the impossible stabilization of cotton.

There are a number of proposals for regional stabilization funds, which while they would exceed national funds, would neither address the issue of weak performance by the cotton sector due to high cost structures, nor solve the problem of inadequate price risk management. Even though it is true that regional stabilization funds could provide a better cushion than national funds against more profound shocks, it is clear that their existence will not prevent these shocks from happening. Further, as in the case of National Facilities, Regional Stabilization Funds can be a source of irrational expectation by markets, and their management can create significant governance problems. It simply provides additional liquidity without questioning the sustainability of these schemes.

What Can't Seed Cotton Pricing Schemes Do?

No price formula, even if it reflects totally and immediately price variations of international markets, is enough to ensure sustainability of the cotton sector. Seed cotton price variations cannot adjust to all the costs of the cotton sector, which include several other components of some significance. The sustainability of a cotton sector requires taking a look at its global competitiveness, which, in turn, is a question of competitiveness at any given moment and for each type of activity.

However, seed cotton prices are often adjusted in such a way as to send market signals to producers. In WCA, the seed cotton price represents the main cost of cotton lint. Further, this price is usually negotiated each year, based on the sector's results and the bargaining power of producers. For that reason, seed cotton price often serves as a tool to adjust the competitive gap.

However, an adjustment using the price of seed cotton is not always possible. In most countries of the region, producers and ginners prefer using a price formula negotiated by the parties (or sometimes imposed by the government) before the season starts, rather than negotiate *a posteriori* how the season's revenues will be shared. This preference shows clear risk aversion. For producers and ginners, the idea is to come up with a forecast of revenues and share the burden of risk before the season starts. In real terms, price formulas integrate the bargaining power of the market's different stakeholders, including the role of the government.

The more rigid the price formula is, the higher the commercial risk supported by the ginner. Conversely, the more flexible the price formula is, the higher the commercial risk supported by the producer. Some price formulas do not link seed cotton revenues to cotton fiber prices on international markets (example: the price formula in the 2004 protocol in Burkina Faso). Yet, when seed cotton prices do not follow international indexes, commercial risk is *a priori* low for the producer and high for the ginner who has certain liabilities but unknown revenues. Conversely, if a price formula reflects directly and fully variations in cotton fiber prices on international markets, the lower the commercial risk—*a priori*—for the ginner and the higher for the producer.

In the Cotton-4, commercial risk is a financial risk, whether supported by the producer or the ginner. When the cotton sector takes a hit, the effects are felt whether the sector is still public or has been privatized. Nearly one-third of the working population works in some aspect of cotton production, and the cotton sector is the chief source of revenues in these countries. Thus, it is critical that Cotton-4 Governments seek to anticipate and limit the risk to their respective budgets by putting in place monitoring and incentive systems that will compel producers and ginners to carefully measure the commercial risks ahead of them each season and to elaborate a sound and efficient system for sharing these risks.

How Can the Risks Associated with Transport be Reduced?

Logistics and transport are critical for improving the efficiency of the cotton chain because of their direct costs and the risks they involve. Direct transport costs account for approximately 15 percent of FOB price.[11] Indirect costs and risks are potentially more costly and damaging for the cotton chain. Any risk will be charged at the maximum cost it could possibly result in. Inefficient rural transport can seriously impede seed cotton quality, and in extreme cases be a disincentive for producers to cultivate cotton. Moreover, inefficient export transport can lead to delayed deliveries and even missed deliveries and consequently has a high risk to reputation. Transport is an element of the supply chain with a very specific risk (hold-up risk). If transport is not carried out in a timely manner, honoring the terms of the seed cotton contract and/or delivery of cotton fiber, the ginner can suffer serious penalties. In the event that the ginner is unable to honor his contract with a trader, he risks losing his credibility, damaging his reputation and being asked to reduce prices on future deliveries. In the worst-case scenario, (if the client is from the textile industry), the ginner risks losing the client.

To mitigate transport's effects on the commodity chain, the trade-off between risk and price must be carefully weighed when selecting a transport company. In this region, in which professional transport companies may be hard to come by, second best options may have to suffice. Indeed, high transport quality in the current economic and institutional environment is extremely costly. However, if transport quality is completely disregarded, hold-up risks are extremely high and indirect costs may end up exceeding savings on the transport price (direct costs).

Issues and solutions are different for rural and export transport. However, the underlying factors of transport profitability are similar and must be taken into account when making a decision in this area. Transport profitability mainly depends on market structure and price, load percentage, unofficial costs and road maintenance.

---

11. It includes rural transport, export transport and rural roads maintenance.

Rural Transport and the Risk that Seed Cotton Collection in Remote Areas Will End

Rural transport is aimed at collecting seed cotton from fields or warehouses and taking it to ginning factories. The most severe risk associated with inefficient or unprofitable rural transport is that seed cotton will no longer be collected in the most remote areas. If collection were to cease, cotton production would decrease and the incidence of poverty in most remote areas would rise. Today, collection distance and road maintenance varies from country to country in WCA, which means that rural transport costs range between CFA F65 and CFA F142 per trip (SOFRECO 2000).

Three types of actions could be undertaken to improve rural transport:

– Transporters should increase loads by integrating inputs and seed cotton transport,
– Offered transport price should cover parts of fixed costs,
– The State should not neglect maintenance of rural roads.

The rationalization of loads, which requires integrating the transport of inputs and seed cotton, is critical. It was calculated in 2000 that, if rationalized, Cotton Mali's transport fleet could have saved CFA F162 million (SOFRECO 2000). On this note, if transport were outsourced, medium-term contracts between ginners and transport companies would help ensure an increased load percentage.

Transport rationalization is more likely to happen once transport companies have achieved a certain degree of professionalism and, consequently, a critical mass. Individual transporters are less able to rationalize loads.

Except for in the most remote regions, credible private operators may be interested in transporting rural cotton under two conditions:

– the price offered should be able to cover a part of the fixed costs, which means that in the case of Mali, it should be higher than CFA F65/trip, and
– roads should be sufficiently maintained so that trucks do not deteriorate too rapidly.[12]

Credible private transporters are only interested in this market if the price offered by the ginner is above their breakeven costs. If the ginner offers CFA F100-140 per trip for transport, the cost structure will significantly increase. The current price level of CFA F65 per trip offered for rural transport does not adequately compensate transport companies, the main consequence of which is: the least professional transport companies, who do not bear high fixed costs (with obsolete fleets and typically without transport insurance), are the ones who will provide transport service, along with all the potential risks.

Export Transport and High Hold-up Risks

Export transport is comprised of two legs—regional transport (from a landlocked country to a port) and maritime transport. Mitigating the risks and lowering the costs of export

---

12. The State is usually in charge of maintaining rural roads, which are defined as a public good, critical for social and political purposes.

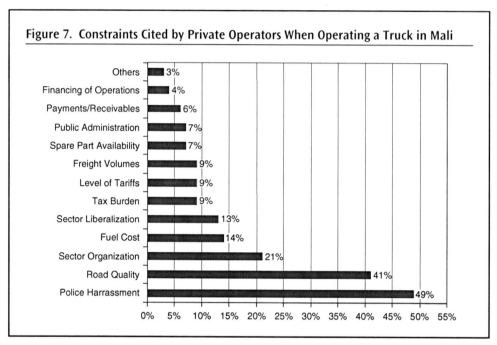

Figure 7. Constraints Cited by Private Operators When Operating a Truck in Mali

Source: Etude pour un service de camionnage plus efficace au Mali, 2003.

transport entails having a good grasp of the economic and institutional environments affecting both legs and controlling for them.

Cotton and transport companies have various risks, interests and constraints:

  – *Cotton companies strive to find reliable, high-quality transport services at the lowest available price.* In WCA, this is a challenge as direct costs for inter-regional transport services are very high for landlocked countries. Maritime costs are also quite expensive because cotton is spontaneously combustible[13], and is therefore classified and charged as a dangerous good (type 4.1 and 4.2 according to the International Maritime Transport Goods code). Indirect costs are also salient. The inefficiency and unreliability of transport services compels cotton companies to stock some of their production in ports to make sure they can honor their contracts with traders. Yet, storage in ports is much more expensive than storage in the factory.
  – *Private transporters face a number of economic and institutional constraints,*[14] such as low traded and imbalanced volumes, high unofficial costs (costly legal and illegal tolls, commonly known as roadblocks), and traffic sharing (see Figure 7 for details).

Imbalanced volumes are the main reason maritime transport costs are so high in the subregion. Exporting small volumes from landlocked countries prevents ginners from

---

13. It also explains why ginners insure their shipments against fire (2 FCFA per kilogramme in Burkina Faso).

14. Insurance costs further increase fixed costs for transport companies.

enjoying scale returns. Along the main trade routes, major shipping lines have recourse to 6000–8000 Twenty-Foot Equivalent Unit (TEU) vessels, but in the subregion they only have 500–1500 TEU vessels, resulting in higher maritime transport costs.[15]

Imbalanced volumes are also a major constraint on inter-regional transport, and may explain why containerization of cotton is low. Today, in countries such as Mali, less than 10 percent of trucks going inland from ports are full. The percentage loaded is consequently very low (less than 50 percent). It is one of the reasons why containerization is so slow to take off in the subregion. Indeed, out of 11,000 containers going to the port, only 2,000 come back full. Inter-regional transport costs are extremely high because Bamako-Dakar transport costs are higher than Europe-Dakar. Consequently, the trucking sector tries to reduce fixed costs as much as possible by delaying investment in its fleets.

In West Africa, inter-regional roads are plagued by informal (mostly illegal) tolls. These so-called roadblocks are the number one complaint of transport companies. This important fact is corroborated by the results of interviews conducted with private operators in Mali, which show that they rank administrative harassment as the largest constraint affecting their operations (Figure 7). In 2003, a pilot study was undertaken to quantify the impact of roadblocks along the main transport corridors of West Africa. Sixty-one drivers took part in the survey.[16] This sample of drivers was stopped more than 2,900 times, which means an average of 48 stops per trip. Drivers had to pay, on average, more than US$200 and waste more than 7 hours at roadblocks each trip. Along the Lomé-Niamey corridor, drivers were stopped 82 times which represents almost one stop every 10 kilometers. Consequently, the average speed of transport vehicles along this corridor can be as slow as 10 kilometers per hour.

Transport companies from landlocked countries may also be particularly affected by higher fuel prices. Mali or Burkina Faso companies may pay fuel 25% higher than in Benin (see Figure 8 for details).

What are the options for lowering export transport costs and risks, and increasing transport quality?

- to lower maritime transport costs, ginning companies must coordinate export transport to ensure larger export volumes, and
- to lower inter-regional transport costs and risks and increase transport quality (where gains are potentially higher and endogenous), a multi-approach strategy must be undertaken:
  - public authorities should facilitate trade by taking measures to reduce roadblock and border-crossing costs,
  - public authorities must enforce professionalism among transport companies,

---

15. Except in regional ports such as Dakar where larger vessels call.
16. A study conducted on various transit corridors in West Africa shows that the average cost of police, gendarmerie and customs harassments ranges from CFA F 100,000 to CFA F 300,000 (about 2,000 US$ to 6,000 US$) for a 20-foot container or, in the case of Mali, anywhere between 8 and 25 percent of the transport cost of a 20 foot container traveling between Abidjan and Bamako (UEMOA 2003).

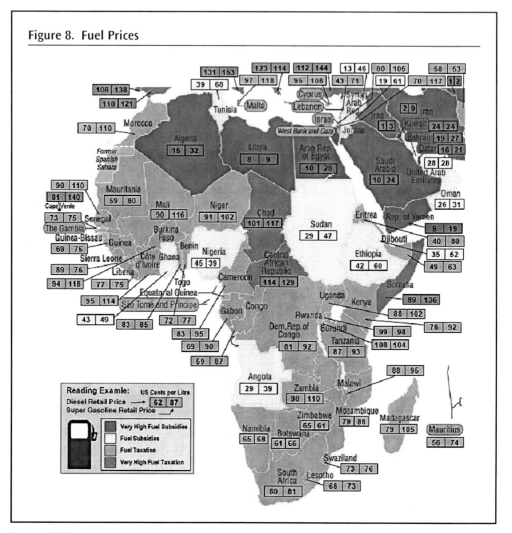

Figure 8. Fuel Prices

Source: GTZ.

  – ginners should be flexible in selecting ports, and when outsourcing, should seek
    to promote professionalism among transport companies by awarding them 2–3
    year contracts, and
  – ginners should explore the possibility of selling ex-ginnery, rather than FOB.

Public authorities could help lower transport costs and risks by easing restrictions. First,
they must address the governance issue, which is key to making transport to and from landlocked countries easier and loss costly. Secondly, authorities must re-examine trucking
industry regulations and institute reforms. Currently, traffic share between transporters in
landlocked counties and transit countries is determined by bilateral transit agreements,
with two thirds consigned to truckers from the landlocked country and one-third to
truckers from the transit country. In WCA, and especially in the landlocked nations, there
is little leeway to select the country's most competitive transport companies. Indeed,

because of the "tour de role" system, where jobs are assigned by rotation, each company with transport union affiliation is guaranteed a certain share of traffic, regardless of the quality of its service or the age of its fleet.[17]

Since the unrest in Cote d'Ivoire, ginners from landlocked countries, notably from Mali, have made great efforts to diversify their trade routes in order to mitigate risks. Flexibility is critical because the average speed can vary tremendously depending on the route and form of transport chosen. For instance, cotton can travel from Bamako to Dakar by rail twice as fast as from Bamako to Conakry by road, even though the former route is 248 kilometers longer (see Table 7 for details).

Transit routes for exporting cotton have become more varied and flexible. In 2002, 71 percent of Mali's cotton exports were shipped via Abidjan, the rest being split between Dakar (14.5 percent) and Lomé (14.5 percent). As Mali swiftly adopted a new, more flexible strategy, cotton export transits to Abidjan plummeted in favor of Lomé (2003–2004) and Dakar (2005). The latter has become Mali's number one port for exporting cotton (36 percent).[18] Another component of Mali's transit diversification strategy is the use of Tema port (Ghana). In 2005, Mali shipped one-fifth of its cotton via this port.

Ginners can foster greater professionalism among transport companies by awarding them 2–3 year contracts and developing stronger links to them. In this regard, countries in the subregion may wish to closely examine and even replicate the experiment being conducted in Burkina Faso (see Box 5).

Ginners should further explore selling ex-ginnery in lieu of FOB,[19] preferably by rail. Savings could be significant—as much as 4.5 billion CFA F for Mali. Traders could then negotiate multiple services, at more competitive rates, with shipping lines. By selling ex-ginnery, cotton companies could shift the burden of export transport to traders.

The Need to Improve the Reliability of Quality and Grading

Improvements in the quality of WCA cotton could have a significant positive impact on the sector. If a regional quality improvement program were implemented in the subregion, the selling price could increase by an estimated 5–6 U.S. cents per pound, which would represent gains of between 55 and 65 US$ million[20] (of which between 8 and 20 million would go to producers) for the cotton sector in the subregion.

A comprehensive regional strategy must be undertaken to rapidly improve cotton quality and grading and thereby improve the reputation of WCA cotton. For decades, increased production and higher yields have been the main priorities of cotton companies in the region. Although quality improvement has been a goal of cotton companies, it has not received the attention and investment needed. The cotton sectors in WCA must now develop awareness, all along the cotton chain, of the importance of reliable grading. The

---

17. See Souley (2001) for details.

18. A major feature is the increased use of rail transport. Shipment of cotton via rail jumped from 34,000 tons in 2002 to 65,000 tons in 2005, and is expected to reach 100,000 tons in 2005.

19. Transport cost per km is 20 CFA F by rail and 32 CFA F by road.

20. These calculations assume only half of price increase resulting from the implementation of the quality program (2.5–3 instead of 5–6 cents per pound).

Table 7. Transport Turnaround Time from/to Mali

		Estimated Turnaround Time Of Trucks, Cars And Containers—2004					
Transport to Bamako/origin	Distance km	Time in ports, incl. waiting time, loading, formalities	Connecting time road or rail	Time for formalities, borders, roadblocks	Time for parking in Bamako and customs clearance	Total turnaround time with loading, repairs	Kms per day in transit
				number of days			
Dakar-road	1,365	5	7	3	6	31	195
Dalar-rail	1,228	3	3	1	2	13	409
Dakar-rail-containers	1,228	1	3	1	2	11	409
Lomé	1,967	5	9	6	6	41	219
Tema	1,973	5	9	6	6	41	219
Conakry	980	5	6	2	6	27	463
Cotonou-gas	2,113	2	8	3	4	28	264
Abidjan-road	1,225	4	6	3	6	28	204

Source: Transitaires, 2004.

Table 8. Diversification of Cotton Export Routes (percent)

	2002	2003	2004	2005
Via Dakar	14.5	19.5	26	36
Via Lomé	14.5	43.5	42	28
Via Ghana	0	29	20	20
Via Cotonou	0	0	0	0
Via Abidjan	71	10	12	16

Source: Amprou (2005).

establishment of a regional quality label is a measure that might contribute to improving quality and reliable grading in the subregion, and by extension, the reputation of WCA cotton. WCA cotton sectors must focus on making dramatic improvements to grading.

The quality of WCA seed cotton is usually good in terms of length but falls short in terms of colour and ripeness (key criteria for quality cotton lint), mainly because of unreliable transport and inadequate warehousing facilities. This is why, a comprehensive strategy to improve quality is needed—one involving ginners, producers, and all major stakeholders, including transporters and researchers. Such strategies are, by their very nature, complicated to carry out.

What Steps Should be Taken to Improve the Reliability of Quality and Grading?

Today, the quality of WCA cotton has a less than stellar reputation for the following reasons:

Box 5: Cross-Shareholding between Cotton Companies and a Transport Company in Burkina Faso

Transportation is a central concern for cotton companies because of the hidden costs and high risks it may create. With the idea of creating a mutually beneficial partnership, SOFITEX and the other cotton companies are developing cross-shareholding with transport companies.

In Burkina Faso, El Hadj Dianguinaba, owner of Soba, a major transportation company, acquired shares in the capital of Faso Coton and Socoma.

This cross-shareholding benefits both parties by creating common interests:

– for the transport company, owning shares in the cotton company contributes to the development of a long-term partnership with a major customer, thereby stabilizing expected revenues in the mid-term and reducing sales risks,

– for the cotton company, selling shares to a transport company means it can expect better quality of services and lower markups from the transport company because the cotton company will guarantee it high transport volumes, which means lowering fixed costs for the transport company.

Source: World Bank, 2005.

- While seed cotton quality has improved (particularly in terms of length), more work is needed.
- At least 10 percent of cotton lint is declared above average quality but is not (ONUDI 2004), which is extremely detrimental to the WCA cotton sector.

There are four main criteria that determine the quality of cotton lint: length, resistance, colour, and ripeness (ONUDI 2004). All other things being equal, traders and spinners pay a higher price for longer, more resistant cotton lint that is white and fully mature.

On average, cotton length seems to be highly satisfactory in WCA. It is worth noting that the introduction of new cotton varieties has enabled increases in the outturn ratio and cotton lint length. However, as far as colour or ripeness, WCA cotton continues to suffer from major problems. Indeed, if cotton bales are inadequately stocked or if maritime transport is delayed by several days, the ripeness index may change and then quality decreases rapidly.

Moreover, cotton lint quality depends not only on the quality of the seed but also on harvesting practices and ginning operations. Indeed, in the field, the first contamination risk occurs when collection is delayed, for example, due to competing cotton and cereal harvests. The later the cotton harvest, the more likely it is that the cotton flower will contain leaf pieces and twigs, or suffer from aphids and other insects (such as the white fly). Collecting cotton in the polyethylene bags that fertilizers come in brings significant risk of contamination; polyethylene threads often slide into the fiber of the cotton. The race for profitable ginning and the necessity to produce long fibers can also introduce contamination issues. Indeed, the longer the fiber, the smaller the shell, which means it will be even more difficult to remove the fiber from the shell without breaking it and damaging the fiber. Industrial and traditional cleaning of cotton fiber aggravates that problem, since re-fermentation of residues takes place.

Yet, one of the most problematic issues is grading. Indeed, in the subregion, it has traditionally been done in a somewhat unprofessional manner: grading is performed manually/visually by lenient inspectors who prefer to avoid conflict. In the end, the quality—superior, inferior or average—is less important than the reliability and standardisation of the grading. If, for instance, 10 percent of country A's production is declared "superior," but, in fact, it is not, the grading of all country A's production comes under suspicion, making all of it less desirable on the world market, regardless of its actual quality. In WCA, around 2 percent of production is graded low quality (see Figure 9 for the example of Mali). Hence, we can assume that "misgrading" is frequent and extremely detrimental for cotton in the subregion. It may explain why cotton produced in WCA is sold at a low price on the world market. The trader or the final user is not ready to pay a higher price for average quality cotton.

Issues pertaining to quality and grading are distinct and demand different solutions.

Cotton Lint Quality. To improve the quality of cotton lint, ginners have to invest in appropriate warehousing facilities wherever cotton lint is stocked and develop partnerships with transporters (and possibly shipping lines), whose role greatly affects the color and ripeness of cotton lint.

Cotton Grading: For improvements in this area, a variety of activities need to be carried out:

Figure 9. Malian Cotton Quality

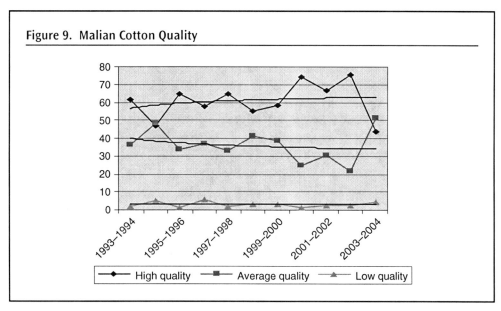

Source: CMDT, 2005.

■ disseminate information regarding grading,
■ reward producers and groups of producers who actually deliver seed cotton with improved quality,
■ develop computerized grading,
■ develop contradictory grading procedures,
■ develop a regional label, which should be strictly enforced, and
■ establish a regional grading laboratory.

Pre-conditions for Establishing Reliable Quality and Grading

Low lint quality is symptomatic of several dysfunctions along the cotton chain. Quality improvement is a collective result. Indeed, cotton lint quality sold to traders mainly depends on (i) seed cotton quality, and (ii) the quality of ginning and export transport. Seed cotton quality alone depends on research, the quality of inputs, cultivation techniques, and the quality of rural transport. Interdependency is so strong that unless all the stakeholders are committed to quality improvement, it is virtually impossible to achieve it.

Grading improvement is a function of political commitment and strategic action on the part of ginners. It occurs when a long-term partnership between ginners and producers has been developed. While political authorities can help—by overseeing the design of a regional label, enforcing the measures adopted, and establishing a regional grading laboratory—responsibility for improving grading falls mainly to the ginners.

Ginners need a critical mass in order to adopt new behaviours and invest in equipment and resources to develop computerized grading.

Moreover, ginneries need to get producers "on board" by cultivating close relationships with them and rewarding them for quality improvements. "Real grading" is a medium-term objective that ginners and producers must agree on and work toward together. Once the ginning companies have completed their information campaign about grading, their next step will be to downgrade part of the production of some producers. If competition is intense among ginners, they will be disinclined to carry out this second step because producers whose cotton lint has been downgraded will immediately look for another ginner less concerned about grading. Consequently, the ginning company dedicated to real grading will loose most of its producers.

CHAPTER 4

Enhancing Sales Revenues

Hela Cheikhrouhou

Volatility is an intrinsic characteristic of commodity markets, such as cotton. Consequently, poorly designed sales strategies that do not adequately manage price risk can undermine efforts to increase yields, improve cost structures and enhance grading. Enhancing sales revenues must be a component of the global strategy to improve the WCA cotton sector's competitiveness. In present day sales strategies in the Cotton-4 are poor to non-existent, particularly in ginning operations that are publicly controlled or held by local private participants, and this is a considerable source of inefficiency for the region's cotton sector. A sound sales strategy should be based on optimizing the ginning company's net margin against its breakeven cost. To do that, ginners must be able to analyze their cost structure in depth and carefully select their counterparts. They should also be able to use a wide range of available cotton contracts and adopt new sales techniques, such as on-line auctions, which have proven to boost sales revenues. In order to design and implement effective sales strategies, cotton companies need the capacity and incentives to behave pro-actively, which are lacking in most WCA countries—even when the sector has been partially privatized.

Privatization will not cure poor sales management and subsequent fiscal risk unless governments design privatization schemes to attract solid, long-term investors. If the government decides to privatize, it may be suitable to target international strategic investors (rather than local investors, for instance), who have the expertise and financial strength to deal with intraseasonal and interseasonal volatility. In addition, these investors will introduce best international practices to sales management, provided the government establishes the right incentives, to ensure that the optimization of local ginning performance does not suffer from investor's global performance optimization. Among possible strategies to align international investors' incentives with those of the key domestic stakeholders, one could cite minority equity position for producers association.

Governments should continue to push for the creation of a World Cotton Futures exchange. Financial markets are incomplete, as they do not currently provide perfect hedging instruments for non-U.S. cotton. However, the increasing volume of exported non-U.S. cotton provides hope for the successful development of a world cotton future contract.

The Challenges of Managing Cotton Price Risk

Ginners in WCA have to manage their sales within volatile markets, both for cotton prices and foreign exchange rates. Cotton is priced in dollars by the demand side of the market, which is its main driver. Yet the bulk of ginners' costs have to be paid in local currency (CFA F), which in turn is pegged to the EUR.[21]

The risk of €/US$ variability can be mitigated using existing financial instruments. The markets for forwards, futures and options instruments are deep and highly developed. Ginners can easily incorporate such instruments into their contractual agreements with traders.

Unlike the case of the United States, and more recently Chinese, cotton (see Box 6), there is currently no organized exchange or OTC market with a perfect hedge against risk for the price of WCA cotton lint. Contrary to a €/US$ currency transaction, which is identical no matter what the seller and buyer's country is, the pricing of a cotton lint transaction depends significantly on the origin of the commodity, its announced quality, the track record of that origin, etc. Consequently, the future price of a bale of cotton lint varies according to its quality and country of origin. The New York Cotton Exchange is the only financial market to offer futures and options contracts in relatively meaningful volumes.

Hence, cotton sales pricing and risk management in the other countries are handled by referring to a proxy, the Cotton Outlook index (see Box 7), known as the "Cotlook," and then adding to or subtracting from it an estimated price differential based on the difference in quality. Cotlook indices are simply indicative quotes reflecting the sales price that cotton intermediaries (traders) intend to charge to mills.

Basis risk between WCA and U.S. origins is significantly high. Ginners in WCA export almost all their production so the price of their origins is more sensitive to international demand than the origins of countries that sell a significant part of their production domestically (United States and Greece). Uzbekistan, for example, has the same export orientation, which explains the strong co-movement of WCA-Uzbek origins and the relatively low co-movement of WCA and U.S. origins. The latter, also a measure of basis risk, explains why the NYCE futures market is not an effective hedging solution (Baffes & Ajwad 2001.) This is further illustrated in Figure 10 below. The basis between any two given cotton origins changes over time, as it also reflects a shift in spinners' demand for specific qualities and the reputation of a specific country or ginner in terms of ability to deliver the promised quality of product.

There have been many (failed) attempts to organize cotton exchanges because the use of a proxy for price is less than ideal (by definition), and the basis risk is high. Brazil created

---

21. €1 = CFA F655.957 (legacy of the FRF 1 = CFA F100). Ginners are also exposed to the risk of devaluation/revaluation of the CFA F vs. €, but this is beyond the scope of this paper.

Box 6: Active Cotton Markets

The New York Cotton Exchange (NYCE) is currently the most active organized exchange for cotton lint. For cotton lint of a specific set of qualities, there are futures contracts and options on futures for up to 18 months. Most of the time, the futures curve tends to be upward sloping.[22] The main constraint for expansion of the volume and coverage of this exchange is it has to be U.S. cotton that is physically delivered at maturity. Therefore, sellers and buyers with cotton from other origins can only use the U.S. futures market as a proxy, to lock in a future level of U.S. cotton price, knowing that they would need to unwind their position before maturity to avoid facing the contractual obligation of physical cotton delivery.

The most actively traded contract, a middling, is the cotton quality on which U.S. policymakers base their various subsidies/incentives to U.S. cotton producers. Specifically, U.S. producers are continuously arbitrating between the U.S. government's subsidies[23] and the NYCE futures market, in order to monetize abnormalities in price behaviors (what is called the "pop" strategy). This means that one of the key drivers of NYCE futures prices is the intricacy of the U.S. subsidies system, a good understanding of which is a pre-requisite for participants who wish to enter the market. For example, the fact that U.S. producers have an implicit free put option[24] from the U.S. government at AWP puts a limit to the downside potential of NYCE futures prices and/or the value of out-of-the-money put contracts, since there will always be a point beyond which it becomes better to sell to the U.S. government.

Besides the U.S. cotton producers, commodity hedge funds have recently emerged as another force actively intervening on the NYCE. Hedge funds thrive on volatility and typically commodities are more volatile than securities, currencies or interest rates. There is, therefore, a need to understand and be able to factor-in the impact of this new category of players, which are difficult to predict, but at the same time add to the liquidity/turnover of the market.

Zhengzhou Commodity Exchange is a promising new cotton futures market. China is an increasingly important player on the international cotton scene, mostly due to its prosperous textile industry. As the single largest consumer of cotton lint, with its own share of local cotton production, it was only natural that a futures market would emerge, especially given the appetite of wealthy investors to speculate on the future trends of the price of cotton. The Zengzhou cotton futures market was created in 2004. Most international cotton market participants predict a bright future for this market. Its main downside for now is that it is intentionally restricted to Chinese nationals. As such it is not accessible to European cotton traders or to WCA ginners. If this constraint is lifted, and if the futures contracts are settled in cotton delivered to China but not necessarily produced in China, then this might represent an interesting sales management alternative for part of the production of WCA ginners.

---

a future market, which suffers from low liquidity. Another attempt has been made in India without much success. NYCE in 1992, and more recently Euronext in 2002, tried and failed to launch a "world" cotton future contract, to respond to the request of producers/ginners worldwide for a hedging instrument that responds better to their needs and corresponds to their main cotton quality. The main reasons mentioned for Euronext failure are: 1) the cost of setting up quality control laboratories at the delivery ports that were selected;

---

22. This curve shape reflects a "positive cost of carry", due to warehousing, insurance, and interest costs, which means that the term structure of cotton prices at date t reflects that prices further out in the future tend to be higher. Also see paragraph 210 and figure 9.

23. The primary objective of US government subsidies is to support the US cotton production, but a by-product of these subsidies is the impact they have on NYCE futures contracts activity and pricing.

24. A put option is a financial contract that gives its holder (here the US producers) the right, but not the obligation, to sell the underlying (here the cotton lint) at a predetermined price to the option seller (here de facto the US government), which will be valuable if market prices drop below that predetermined price.

Box 7: Cotlook A—The Proxy for WCA Cotton's Market Price

The "Cotton Outlook" (Cotlook) index is the cornerstone of sales management for WCA cotton ginners. It started as a publication about the cotton industry, and evolved over time into a powerhouse in the cotton industry, publishing daily much awaited Cotlook indices. To decide on a fixed forward sale price, cotton merchants and WCA ginners would look to Cotlook A's recent quotes and to the NYCE futures and make a judgment on the premium/discount to be added for cotton from that specific origin in that specific tenor/maturity.

The Cotlook index is an indicative quote that estimates the pricing of the nearest cotton lint shipment[25] to spinners. As such, it is derived from Cotlook staff's best judgment, which is based on feedback from a set of cotton traders about the level at which they intend/would be willing to sell specific origins, and takes into account the NYCE closing levels, as well as any publicly available information about actual transactions (the Seam OTC inter-traders platform, any cotton auctions where ginners publish their result such as Jordan, etc.).

The A index is computed as the (un-weighted) average of the 5 cheapest cotton types among 19. Only two West African cottons are allowed to be in the index's 5 cheapest. Until recently, the main reference for the A index was the North Europe (NE) component, but more recently, a Far East (FE) component was introduced to reflect the reality of significantly higher cotton flows to Asia than to Europe.

The main downsides of the Cotlook Index are that it provides only an indicative price, i.e. it is not possible to buy or sell the index spot or forward, and it is susceptible to manipulation. It is not tradable nor can its composition be replicated since the exact formula used to arrive at it is unknown. The only emerging trend is to buy/sell the index "on call," which means that the published value of the index will be used, on a future date, as a basis for pricing the settlement of a contract. Moreover, given the large sums of money staked to it, the index is susceptible to manipulation, despite the Cotlook staff's best intentions and their precautions to reach a fair value.

Finally, it is important to highlight that the Cotlook index and NYCE are inter-dependent. Specific components of the U.S. government subsidies to its cotton producers are derived from the Cotlook A North Europe value, so NYCE reacts indirectly to Cotlook. Conversely, large cotton traders actively use the NYCE to manage their global exposure to cotton price risk, which means that the prices they offer WCA ginners are highly correlated with the performance of the NYCE.

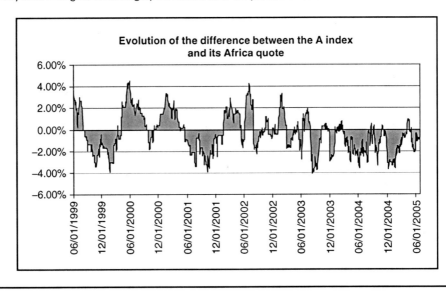

---

25. It is worth highlighting that every year, typically after January for A index, Cotlook publishes for a while both a current and a forward index, to reflect that there is an overlap between sale of cotton both from current and next seasons.

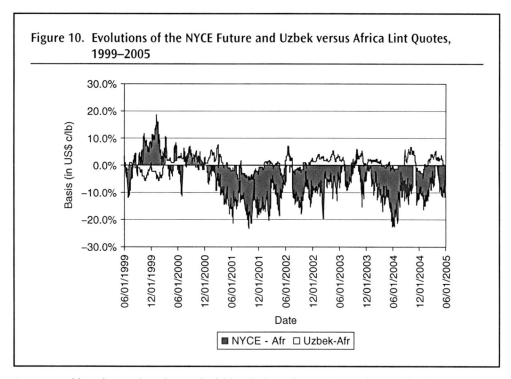

Figure 10. Evolutions of the NYCE Future and Uzbek versus Africa Lint Quotes, 1999–2005

Source: World Bank, 2005 based on Cotlook historical Database and NYCE futures historical quotes.[26]

2) doubts as to the possibility of reaching a critical turnover (this seems to be less of a problem now than a few years ago given the growth of exported cotton from non-U.S. origins); 3) the fear of a boycott from cotton traders who have turned the lack of a perfect hedge into a competitive advantage and a way to increase revenues (there is no consensus on this argument). The Euronext initiative was, however, very close to a successful launch.

As the volume of non-U.S.-exported cottons increases, much effort has been devoted to the design of OTC platform (such as the Seam) and new instruments. The Seam is a web-based trading platform on which cotton traders buy/sell fixed-price or on-call cotton lint contract, including WCA origins, and occasionally cotton swaps (exchange a fixed price for an on-call). The database of the Seam actual transactions would be very informative for WCA ginners, but traders are reluctant to share such info, or to allow ginners to be active counterparts on the Seam. Any attempt to force publication of data or ginners inclusion would probably result in traders deserting the Seam platform to resume more informal media (phone, fax, and so forth). Finally, specialized investment and commercial banks offer their clients with structured cotton derivative contracts, which can help cover a specific

---

26. We used NYCE nearby contract future as a proxy given that A index is based on nearby shipments. There are no public statistics on selling prices for Uzbeck & WCA origins, so "Uzbeck" and "Africa" are the generic quotes for these origins published by Cotlook for its Index A NE. There is no precise formula for "Africa" growth, it is based on a 9 origins basket. Cotlook database has significant gaps in terms of several days where quotes are not available or do not move, i.e. are not updated. Also, historical data is available only for the old index A Northern Europe, as Far East was introduced in 2004.

risk but have the disadvantage of being costly to unwind, so they are typically used as a hedge to be held till maturity. Specialized investment bankers are willing to "slice and dice" the price risk management tools for their clients, and would take care of creating their own synthetic hedges based on the existing financial markets. The limitation here is the banker's appetite for counterpart risk of his client, as well as the banker's own capacity to warehouse and manage structured cotton derivatives.

Given the weak institutional capacity and limited capital base of most WCA ginners, it is highly unwise encourage them to intervene directly on the NYCE anytime soon. In addition to NYCE being an imperfect hedge, futures trading by WCA ginners should not even be considered until all of the steps and tools detailed in sections 2 and 3 have been fully implemented and internalized by WCA ginning companies. Cotton futures markets are volatile, and their liquidity is limited enough to make them vulnerable to large transactions from market participants. It is not advisable to expose WCA ginners to the insolvency risk that could stem from large margin calls on the NYCE futures market. Many WCA ginners wouldn't actually be strong enough financially to be eligible to trade on the NYCE futures market.

Tools for Selling Cotton and the Capacity to Use Them Proactively

Within the context outlined above, of volatile and incomplete financial markets for cotton, WCA ginners have a number of tools to help them with cotton sales. Specifically, the specialized cotton intermediaries—the traders—offer an increasingly wide array of cotton lint contracts to choose from, with varying levels of flexibility and embedded risks. Moreover, cotton sales are typically over-the-counter (OTC)[27] transactions that can be bilateral, with the advantage of personalized market feedback, or multilateral (either fax-based or web-based auctions) with the advantage of increased transparency in the process. Ginners have also to choose and manage exposure to the right mix of counterparts, either professional intermediaries (traders) or end-consumers of cotton lint (spinners). Finally, ginners need to have a minimal institutional capacity to support cotton sales management.

The Range of Cotton Lint Sales Contracts

Traders offer an array of contracts[28] with varying degrees of price flexibility but also embedded risks that ginners have to understand thoroughly. Specifically, while price risk is eliminated in fixed-price forwards, it remains flexible in on-call contracts. While the ginner will incur passively those risks in automatic deferred fixing contracts, he can actively manage them when he has the option to choose the fixing time, and can limit his exposure to downside risk through minimum-price guarantees. The risks are, however, amplified when the

---

27. OTC transactions are negotiated privately as opposed to being carried out through an organized exchange or public market.

28. There are no explicit costs or commissions related to using a specific type of contracts, except when it involves the purchase of a minimum price guarantee (as will be detailed hereafter); rather, ginners need to successfully negotiate favorable contractual agreements, in terms of transparency of the price fixing mechanism–if the contract has a flexible sale price- and level of the price (if forward sale) or premium/discount (if flexible sale based on an external reference).

ginner gives the trader the option to choose the time of fixing, and when the ginner enters into a contract that is on call off the NYCE.

Traditional Fixed-price Forwards. While detailed data is not available, it is estimated that more than 80 percent of WCA cotton lint production is sold through fixed price forward contracts. This is also the most frequently used type of contract worldwide. These are generally "regular" FOB contracts, with fixed price in €/kg, or occasionally US$/kg. In WCA, ginners sell with tenors of up to one year. Traders would be willing to quote them forward for tenors of up to three years.

In order to allow ginners to cash in proceeds of their sales upon departure of trucks or stuffing of containers in their gin yard, traders offer "Ex-gin" or "Delivered warehouse" forward sales. Depending upon the efficiency of their invoicing department, this solution enables ginners to save up to three months of financing costs. Traders are very interested in this alternative as it enables them to effect a proper selection of the goods they have to ship/buy. In spite of the economic edge this type of contract could offer to the ginners, they have not been used much in WCA.

On-call Contracts. In on-call contracts, the price is established as a variable to be fixed at anytime during the life of the contract, determined as a discount or premium versus an external market reference, usually the A index, the Africa component of the index or the NYCE futures. Statistics are not available on the WCA cotton volume sold using on-call contracts, but interviews with most trading industry participants point to ad hoc usage depending on market conditions and ginners views over the last couple of years. Although on-call NYCE offers easier hedging possibilities, WCA ginners are rightfully reluctant to use New York futures as a reference and are much more comfortable with the A index, which has a significantly lower basis risk vs. their origins.

Traders offer various price fixing possibilities, for example, 50 percent at buyer's call, and 50 percent at seller's call. In these contracts, ginners have to develop the capacity to proactively monitor the markets over the life of the on-call contract and have a clear strategy on what is a desirable market level to start fixing prices. There is a drawback to conceding the right to traders to fix the price for 50 percent of the volume sold. Indeed, traders usually know better how to choose the best time to exercise their option, that is, when the market is considered underpriced.[29]

On-call contracts with deferred automatic price fixing for regular and small quantities have the advantage that they allow ginners to accompany the market and average out their sales price. Here they cannot wait and speculate for too long. In a way, they are forced to sell and not postpone each time. The fixing choice is taken out of the hands of the ginner and trader. The disadvantage is that ginners using these contracts are passively replicating the average of the market, rather than proactively setting the price.

On-call basis off NYCE contracts can be made more attractive with the minimum guaranteed price feature (prix minimum garanti or PMG). PMG contracts offer the ginner

---

29. Moreover, while traders can manage their exposure in an on-call contract by shorting the cotton ahead of a likely ginner-enacted price fixing if they think the market is overpriced, ginners cannot create new long cotton positions to mitigate the risk of an unfavorable trader-enacted price fixing.

the chance to benefit from upside potential in the NY market, while protecting him from the downside. This is because the contract includes an at-the-money forward "put" option, which is charged to the ginners at cost price. This is an option to sell the cotton at the forward price that was prevalent at the beginning of the contract; the ginner can exercise this option at any point during the life of the contract, even if the market has dropped in the meantime. Traders mention an option cost of 2–4 cents per pound on NYCE, to be compared with annual cotton price volatility of 20–30 cents per pound, in effect, options allow for substantial flexibility with a limited cost.

PMG presents the disadvantage that the minimum guaranteed price is always lower than the equivalent forward contract's price because of the option cost, and the ginner remains exposed to basis risk The ginner remains exposed to a substantial basis risk between Cotlook A (or Africa Cotton reference) and NYCE futures. Traders do offer various tailoring possibilities to mitigate the cost and risks of these contracts.[30]

Euro-Dollar Risk Protection. If ginners wish to fix only the US$/kg but not the €/US$ to benefit from potential future weakening of €/US$, traders can embed a protection from €/US$ appreciation. €/US$ derivatives markets are cheaper and deeper than cotton's. This might be a better solution for WCA countries than for example what was observed in early 2005 when ginners were selling in US$ (reflecting an expectation of EUR weakening, which may or may not happen). Detailed statistics on the volumes that ginners have chosen to sell is US$ in 2005 are not available, but appear to be limited.

OTC Sales Techniques

In the absence of accessible and effective organized exchanges, WCA ginners sell their cotton OTC, either by one-on-one phone calls or fax auctions. A promising channel is web-based auctions. Bilateral contact between ginners, traders and spinners will remain important and continue to be one of the main selling techniques. This is because it motivates traders to tailor their contract proposals to ginners, provide ongoing market analysis and even free on-the-job trainings and workshops. In the case of spinners, it personalizes the supplier-consumer relation.

Online auction is emerging as a complementary, low-cost-high-reward OTC sale technique but one which requires a critical amount of committed supply to discourage boycotts by traders, as proven by the recent experience in Brazilian cotton sales. Online cotton auctions have a long track record in the U.S. market. Moreover, in Guatemala, coffee has been successfully sold through online auctions. This technique is far superior to Mali's fax-based auctions, where bidders have to maintain prices for 24 hours, which is too long and very risky; therefore, bidders tend to under-price the cotton to create a cushion against adverse market fluctuations. The Seam is the leader in online auctions and has successfully

---

30. The PMG contract can be tailored to the ginner's limited ability to incur option cost. It is possible to have "collar" structures, where the ginner pays a lower cost for downside protection, but benefits only from partial upside. Also, traders can allow the ginner to have a PMG contract whose tenor exceeds that of the physical contract delivery: in a contract with April/May delivery of cotton but with PMG maturing in November, the ginner can continue to benefit from potential upside while not incurring the warehousing, insurance and financing costs of cotton.

Table 9. Pros and Cons of Each Type of Cotton Lint Contract

Type of contract	Pros	Cons
Fixed price forward contract	▨ No more exposure to price volatility (lock-in margin) ▨ Upward sloping forward price curve gives premium to long term sales ▨ Long forwards can help reduce exposure to inter-seasonal price volatility ▨ Serves as collateral to access bank financing	▨ No more potential for participation in upside price movement. ▨ Exact cotton qualities and volumes are not known for certain well in advance ▨ If seed cotton cost is linked to actual market average, ginner's margin is exposed to market's upward moves.
On-call contract	▨ Serves as collateral to access bank financing without ginner forced to fix price if market unfavorable. ▨ Sale made while price remains flexible to be fixed anytime in contract life.	▨ Remain exposed to market deterioration. ▨ Exposed to basis risk, especially if on-call is basis off NYCE. ▨ If price fixing is 50% ginner-50% trader's option, ginner always loses out a bit, as trader is better able to lock-in market lows.
Minimum guarantee price (PMG)	▨ Limits exposure to market deterioration, while keeping potential to participate in upside. ▨ "Guarantee" cost can be reduced if ginner willing to limit participation in upside (collar structure) ▨ Can be offered by traders in €/kg, so PMG level locks in foreign exchange as well.	▨ Only available for on-call NYCE contract, thus significant basis risk remains. ▨ Not viable financially for ginners with breakeven above market. ▨ Requires close monitoring to choose fixing time.
Automatic price fixing	▨ Approximate market average, useful especially if final seed cotton cost is linked to it.	▨ Passive, takes selling decision out of ginner's hands, thus can lead to passive replication of downward trend.
US$ contract with flexibility to fix €/US$	▨ Increased flexibility, no need to decide simultaneously on both cotton and currency price fixing. ▨ Financial markets offer a wide range of €/US$ price risk hedging instruments. ▨ Ginner can access €/US$ hedging indirectly using trader's creditworthiness.	▨ Fixing parameters have to be transparent to avoid hidden costs. ▨ Requires close monitoring to choose fixing time.

implemented an online cotton auction in Brazil despite staunch resistance from traders. A way to mitigate this risk could be to have a WCA regional auction site and a clear commitment from all ginners to sell a minimum percentage (for example, 35 percent of annual production) through the online auction.[31]

The online auction of the Seam has embedded features that can also help with counterpart risk management, a crucial subject. The sanctity of contracts is crucial in the cotton industry. The prevailing perception of counterpart risk is that traders are exposed to WCA ginners, but ginners are equally exposed to default from traders or spinners.[32]

Counterpart Risk Management

Ginners need to formalize the criteria for counterpart eligibility: run basic financial soundness checks, set counterpart limits by tenors and amounts, and monitor the utilization of these limits. Limits monitoring should take into account the pre-settlement exposure due to contract mark to market (MTM).[33] Clearly, the old practice of 100 percent of agency sales through one trader is suboptimal.

WCA ginners need to improve substantially their follow-up on contract execution. Right now, traders often do not need working capital to buy from African ginners, since they often get paid for their sales to spinners before having to pay back the ginner. This trader "perk" is the result of bad organization in the sales departments of ginners.[34] A way to eliminate this risk is to have an effective control for contracts delivery in the ginning company. Moreover, WCA ginners sometimes do not negotiate with traders the cost of carry, charging the same price for early shipments as delayed. Some traders delay contract execution by up to 12 months so as to avoid unfavorable market prices. This is effectively a case of default. It is important to select carefully agreed upon counterparts with a good track record of settling contracts.

Building Institutional Capacity

The lack of incentives promoting proactive use of sales management tools, along with limited analytical capacity or authority to make decisions, can prove quite damaging to sales performance. For example, for five years, Central Asian Ginners used the on-call contract with 50 percent at ginner option,[35] and never took the initiative to fix

---

31. In terms of costs, the Seam perceives a small transaction fee per contract sold through its auction system, the magnitude of which would be confirmed if the WCA countries decide to adopt this technique. As an indication, one can use the current fees for the online auctions of Brazil, US cotton producers as well as inter-traders.

32. As it turns out, spinners are typically riskier counterparts than ginners. Traders would not be willing to assume spinners' risk in a one or two year contract, as this would present a high default risk. Typically sales to spinners are made in tenors up to six months. Even cotton traders are mostly mid-size (relative to international standards) family-owned businesses, with no credit rating and no open capital.

33. If a ginner sells at a high fixed price, and then the market drops, the likelihood of his counterpart defaulting increases.

34. Burkina Faso is held up as a model of good contract follow-up. Mali has improved significantly over the last 18 months.

35. This refers to options where up to 50 percent of the amount can be fixed at the ginner's initiative, anytime prior to delivery date (typically 2–8 months).

before maturity, always letting it be automatically fixed at expiration. This shows a fear of initiative-taking and personal liability least the wrong timing is chosen. This lack of initiative and shunning of personal responsibility has led to cases where up to 100,000 tons of the same cotton with various traders has matured on the same day, possibly moving the market.

There is a need to reduce the centralization of decision making in WCA by having a sales team. For example, ginners could have at least two layers of management that are closely involved in sales contracts to ensure some stability and institutional memory.

However, the ginning companies have to be of a certain minimum size to absorb the administrative cost of employing quality sales management staff. If the industry is atomized, the cost becomes prohibitive and outsourcing or pooling, which is sub-optimal, has to be considered. These issues must be taken into account when designing a privatization scheme for the ginning operations in a country.

A key area for capacity building is training. Quality training is only useful if given to the right people—those who have passed a pre-training test (in technical matters and in English). Courses should be provided in cotton school (Memphis, Liverpool, and so forth), as well by traders and investment banks. It would be useful to make contractual agreements with trainees whereby the company commits to keeping them for at least 2 years, and they, in return, would develop concrete proposals on how to apply their training to formulate their company's sales strategy. Donors could finance this type of educative process, along with English language courses.

Designing and Implementing a Sales Strategy

In WCA countries, cotton companies' sales strategies tend to be passive or non-existent, which is a more speculative approach to sales management. As pricetakers on the international cotton market, and operating in a volatile and tight margin environment, WCA ginners are supposed to be conservative in their sales management to secure their financial viability. Their noted absence of formal sales management strategies and their "wait-and-see" attitude in periods of peak market volatility may achieve just the opposite result.

When it comes to designing a sales strategy, one size can never fit all. Sales strategies vary depending on the type of company, the incentives that shape its rationality, and its ability to react wisely to market moves. Public companies may have to pursue a different objective than private companies, which aim to maximize return on equity (ROE) under the constraints of their cost structure, capital endowment, and cash-flow projections. Governments and donors may distort the rationale of private companies by stepping in with financial support.

The basic rationale of a sales strategy consists of setting performance objectives that are in line with the company profile. Large international strategic investors may have higher performances objectives than small-scale investors, as they are operating worldwide and arbitrating between the most rewarding investments. This means that they might be more demanding in terms of minimum profitability, but also more capable of designing and implementing a successful sales strategy. Much will depend on what governments have set as targets for the sector's privatization (see Chapter 5).

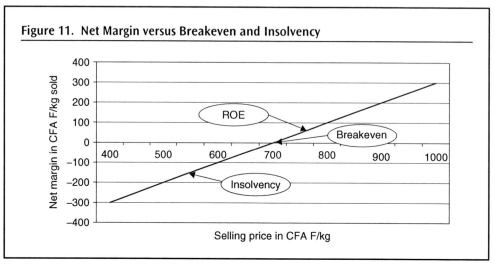

Figure 11. Net Margin versus Breakeven and Insolvency

Source: World Bank, 2005.

Set Realistic Performance Objectives

Ginners need the following pre-requisites in terms of a Management Information System:

■ Have a strong analytical accounting system, able to estimate in a very detailed manner the different costs incurred per unit produced, specifically the conversion costs.[36]

■ Maintain up-to-date estimates of expected seed cotton volume to be purchased, by quality and expected pick-up date, and accordingly estimates of timing and volume of finished products (cotton lint).

If the pre-requisites are met, the ginner's Finance and Sales manager can then derive a parameter that will be crucial to the sales management process: the breakeven cost (BEC) per unit of cotton lint. This cost is the sum of the seed cotton cost[37] and the conversion cost. Each CFA F of sale price per unit made above the BEC contributes to building the annual profit objective. Conversely, sales made below the BEC generate a loss that reduces the ginner's capital (see Figure 11). For a given production volume, the manager can estimate the average sale price per unit that enables him to achieve the ROE objective and the average sale price per unit that corresponds to complete insolvency (loss equals capital). Finally, the more robust the projected production BEC, the more visibility the ginner would have to sell over longer horizons. Breakeven cost is a dynamic and complex parameter, and requires detailed and thorough a ginner's analytical accounting and tracking of historical and current expenses and cashflows. These would allow to determine with a higher degree

---

36. For example Dunavant's ginning operation in Zambia has a good handle on the conversion cost. It includes all the costs incurred to convert seed cotton into cotton lint: transport, warehousing, financing, administrative and operational costs. At a market price that generates 10-20 cents profit vs. estimated breakeven price, they would hedge through 2–3 years fixed forward sales, thereby locking in a margin that probably reflects their internal ROE.

37. Including any agreed upon *ristourne* formula impact.

of precision the cost of current production and expected costs of upcoming production (based on assumptions that would need to be adjusted dynamically).

The next step in the rationale is to track realized vs. unrealized sales performance in order to guide current year's sales decisions and end-of-year provisioning for inter-seasonal price fluctuations. Having determined the key parameters for the target selling price, the manager will need to track continuously the actual average selling price realized year-to-date on volumes sold for current and next fiscal years (ideally up to two or three years ahead[38]), as well as the current market value of the remaining expected production volume over the same timeframe. This will provide him with accumulated realized profit (or loss) as well as estimated profit (or loss) on unsold production. The latter is known as "open position mark-to-market."[39] The sum of realized earnings and position MTM for the current fiscal year have to be benchmarked vs. the annual ROE objective and level of capital to identify how good or bad the expected financial performance is for the full year. Moreover, at the end of the fiscal year, the estimated open position for the next year should serve as a basis to adjust the provisions for price fluctuation, a mechanism for smoothing the impact of inter-seasonal volatility.

Against the above pattern, the manager will need to determine intermediate "profit taking" and "stop loss" levels—cotton lint price levels that correspond to a net margin that is attractive enough or risky enough to prompt some selling activity. Human nature is such that people tend to be bullish near the market top and bearish near the bottom. In the 2004/05 season, WCA ginners sold only 20 percent of their production between March and December 2004, versus the 80 percent typically sold during that period in other seasons. They preferred to "wait and pray" rather than lock in the loss. Objectively selected trigger levels can avoid ego-driven behavior where one does not want to recognize that the market is proving him wrong. For example, the ginner can decide that each time a key level is triggered, he will sell a determined percentage of his production.

In the specific case of WCA ginners where the sales contracts are collateral crucial to gaining bank financing, this constraint should be internalized in the selling decision. This means that the Finance and Sales manager needs to generate his cash flow projections regularly and identify minimum sales volumes needed per month over a rolling twelve-month horizon. Bank financing will not always be a binding constraint to fix the price/margin, since the manager can occasionally decide to enter into a flexible contract, with special care to have clear price fixing rules.[40]

---

38. For example, Dunavant, conscious that their ginning operation is long Zambian cotton for the foreseeable future, will manage cotton price risk continuously over a horizon of 18–24 months, exceptionally up to 36 months.

39. Cargill's Paraguay ginner, whenever he buys with cash cotton seed from farmers, generally locks-in the net margin by selling on NYCE futures market, while waiting to sell his physical cotton lint, and if he decides not to lock the price on NYCE, has limits on un-hedged open cotton positions.

40. For example, the manager can decide to fix the US$/lint price in the contract but defer the decision to fix the EUR/US$ foreign exchange rate. Similarly, he can keep the US$/lint flexible and fix the premium or discount of the lint origin sold vs. a neutral reference, for example the average of Cotlook's quote for his specific origin, and the Cotlook A index, i.e.:

$P = \dfrac{(katy + A)}{2} - d$ Where P is the flexible price formula, Katy is the lint origin, A is the Cotlook A Far East quote and d is the discount agreed upon in advance. Flexible contracts with minimum price guarantee (usually indexed on NYCE) can be used as collateral for pre-export financing of up to 100 percent of the guaranteed price.

Occasionally, for example on a quarterly basis, the manager should generate a simple and plausible set of stress scenarios to challenge his working assumptions (costs, volumes, prices) and devise risk mitigation actions that would be enacted if the scenario were to become more likely. This is a way to step back from day-to-day management and see the big picture.

Diversify the Set of Counterparts Wisely

Ginners can sell directly to spinners or to traders. Spinners are the end users of lint cotton, while cotton traders are intermediaries between ginners and spinners. Most Cotton-4 cotton is sold through European cotton traders (with the exception of Chad which until recently used to sell exclusively to spinners). There are currently approximately 15 active traders[41] on the African market, but with significant variance in their size, sophistication and market share. As explained in Box 8, pricing competitiveness can vary among traders depending on their internal business strategy, whether they are so called "basis traders" or "flat rate traders." Therefore, ginners need not only to diversify their sales strategy to cover different types of traders, but also to understand the types of traders and what drives them.

For the continuity and financial viability of his business, a ginner should avoid undue concentration of sales through a specific trader, and try to develop some ties with spinners. Spinner loyalty to a specific origin is valuable, since spinners usually try to keep the same cotton mix, unless forced to change due to absence of supplies over a long period of time. The costs to spinners of switching are high so their decisions on mix tend to be long lasting. It is, therefore, important for a ginner to make sure his origin is regularly supplied to its main users.

Tailor the Sales Contract Mix Appropriately

As the Finance and Sales manager goes ahead with the overall strategy to protect equity (try to sell above breakeven) and achieve ROE (lock-in attractive levels), he will have to choose among a mix of contracts with varying degrees of selling price flexibility.

At low market price (around CFA F550-560 per kg), the sales strategy of WCA ginners, who typically have breakeven costs around CFA F650-800 per kg, cannot be the same as for cost-competitive ginners such as those in Brazil and Paraguay (breakeven cost estimated at equivalent CFA F450 per kg). The latter are able to cover their cost at low market prices, and are looking to maximize their profit. Conversely, the WCA ginners are below breakeven so their objective should be to minimize losses and avoid insolvency.

As a result, Brazilian ginners can take more risk with selling strategies, which explains why they use NYCE options more extensively, and even NYCE futures. Options have a cost attached to them, but when WCA ginners are already below their breakeven price, i.e. already in the loss-making zone, they are unwilling to incur additional costs for an uncertain benefit[42], especially if they don't have objective criteria to decide on the best time to exercise the option and lock-in a margin. Managing the level of ginner conversion costs

---

41. In vertical integration between international trader and ginner, sale prices are not set at arm's length, since the trader owns the ginner and can decide which vehicle will be most profitable. Fock also reinforces this position (2005).

42. Both Mali and Burkina Faso have started to use PMG contracts successfully, but in 2004/05 they were reluctant to use them given already largely negative net margins.

Box 8: Basis Cotton Traders versus Flat Rate Cotton Traders

Basis traders typically hedge automatically any new cotton position through an opposite contract on the NYCE, but can also keep some proprietary trading position. A basis trader is best positioned to buy from ginners when futures are on a "good base" i.e. when futures are trading upwards. On the flip side, basis traders will tend to sell to spinners when futures are trading low. There are few pure basis traders.

Flat rate traders mostly transact fixed price forward cotton contracts. They try to hedge back-to-back fixed rate purchases and sales of cotton. Given that it is rare to buy and sell the same origin simultaneously, they tend to hedge using other origins that are either similar (have a stable basis between them) or go long on an origin that is underpriced and/or short on an origin that they believe is overpriced. Flat rate traders also do need to go to the NYCE, but they do it less frequently; it is not at the core of their business model.

Both types of merchants take positions on the basis: typically, they would try to be long on what they consider to be the best value of the day. When hedging open positions in one type of cotton, they look for high degrees of substitution. For example, if a trader buys African cotton and sells Central Asian, this is considered a relatively good hedge as these two cottons display a stable basis/high degree of correlation.

Example of basis vs. flat rate trader:

Assume a basis trader had quoted a mill (spinner) at 5 cents on NY (i.e. NY was at 42 cents and they quoted 47 cents to the mill). So did the flat rate trader.

If NY futures moved up by 10 cents, the basis trader, whose long position moves with NYCE, would now have to make the same quote, i.e. NY + 5 would stand at 57 cents. The flat trader had a fixed cost long position, which means he is not sensitive to NY movements so he could potentially maintain the 47 cents quote, but he would probably take advantage of NY move and win the deal with a bigger margin, e.g. sell at 54 cents.

The difference is due to the fact that when the flat rate trader bought from a ginner at say 43 cents, he kept that long position as is. On the other hand, the basis trader who also bought at 43 cents from a ginner, immediately sold NY as a partial hedge. So when NY moves up, the basis trader loses on his net position/cost.

The difference between Basis trading vs. Flat rate trading only provides a short term competitive advantage one way or another. Later on, cash markets adjust to reflect NY movements. Indeed, the flat rate trader, after selling to the mill, will have to continue his job i.e. buy again from the ginner. In the meantime, cash market (Cotlook A) would have moved/ adjusted so the next purchase cost will be higher.

Source: World Bank, 2005.

efficiently will help lower the breakeven cost, thereby offering more flexibility in sales management strategies.

Traders advise limiting on-call contracts to a maximum of 10–20 percent of total sales and recommend that ginners follow these contracts closely to choose the appropriate time to fix the price, when it is not an automatic deferred fixing. Typically, it takes many years of experience before clients start to use derivatives, and even then, they always miss the best time to exercise their right to fix the price in "on call contracts" (see Figure 12). In the coffee business, for example, roasters tend to buy too high and producers sell too low.

When the cotton seed formula is related to the Cotlook A future average, on-call contracts with automatic deferred fixing can be attractive. These contracts respond to the need to be regularly present on the market, and average out the sale price in terms of being very close to the index's actual future average, but they do not permit the ginner to take a proactive

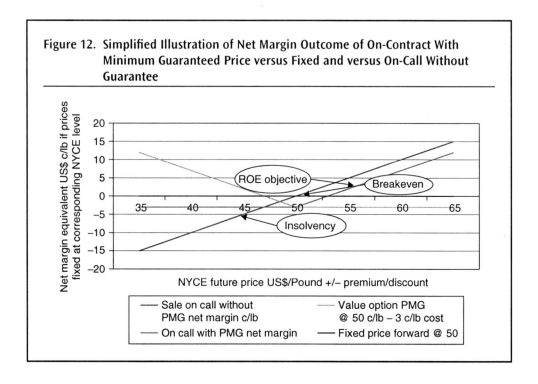

Figure 12. Simplified Illustration of Net Margin Outcome of On-Contract With Minimum Guaranteed Price versus Fixed and versus On-Call Without Guarantee

approach to position management and choose appropriate sales prices to lock-in. However, this can be useful when the ginner has committed to a seed cotton cost formula that links the final cost to the index's future average. In such a scenario, the ginner has a fluctuating cost component that is best hedged through a sales component that mimics that fluctuation.

The NYCE futures curve is generally upward sloping, indicating that—all things being equal—the market assigns a positive cotton cost-of-carry, i.e. the further away the selling date, the higher the price tends to be (Figure 13). In addition to the expectations of market participants' expectations or bets on future spot price, this slope reflects the cost of carrying long cotton positions—warehousing, insurance and financing—which indicates that in most cases, the 1-year forward price for a bale of cotton is higher than its current spot price. This does not mean, of course, that the actual spot price one year later will be necessarily lower than the price locked-in through the future.

Accordingly, a good strategy for minimizing the risk to a ginner's financial viability is to sell long forward when the net margin meets ROE, provided the ginner has reasonable visibility on his breakeven costs and requires ROE over the next three years. Typically, when cotton prices are high, WCA ginners sell maximum one season ahead, while a good practice would be to seize such opportunities to lock in the attractive market peaks for part of forecasted production for two or three years ahead. This requires a good capacity for forecasting future costs. In Brazil/Australia, the ginner is also the producer and knows all the future cost components, so once there is a certain positive margin, he can sell long-term forward, two or three years.

The seed cotton cost formula can have a complex influence on the net margin, and, therefore, on the selling strategy. For example, for 3 consecutive cotton seasons in Mali,

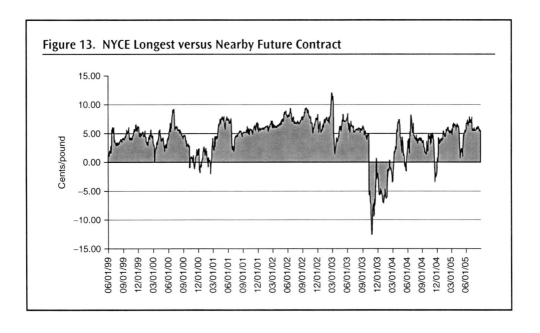

Figure 13. NYCE Longest versus Nearby Future Contract

starting in that of 2005/06, the initial seed cotton price will correspond to a cost component of CFA F160 to 175 per kg. It can be revised if there is a shift in the trends. The final price paid to producers is a fraction of Cotlook A's actual performance over the season. In theory, the safest strategy would be to mimic the Cotlook A average for the corresponding fraction of the sales, i.e. there is a need to sell regularly and avoid long forward contracts. Long forward contracts could be detrimental to ginners if the next-shipment-price goes up, given that the cost of seed cotton remains linked to the average of next-shipments measured in the A index. Another possibility would be to sell on call NY with minimum guaranteed price, but the challenge is to choose the right time to exercise the option given the commitment to do at least as well as the market average. In addition, the basis risk of NYCE versus the A index remains uncovered.

The market conditions on the date that the initial price to producers is set represent a proxy of what ginners could lock-in on that date, to meet that price without losses. However, given that the amount of production is not known with certainty and that it is rarely (if ever) wise to sell most of the expected production at one point in time, ginners would typically have already started hedging for the upcoming season, an element they'll take into account when negotiating the initial price. Once ginners commit to an initial price, they would have to try to protect the corresponding breakeven (shareholders' equity), while aiming to achieve ROE through their sales during the rest of the season.

What Can Governments Do to Enhance Sales Revenues?

The size and institutional capacity of WCA ginners matter more than their public or private status, assuming that, in either case, their sales management will be performed rationally. Effective cotton sales management requires minimal expert staffing and decision-making analytical tools. For example, the overwhelming feedback from the European traders' community

Table 10. Seed Cotton Formula's Impact on a Ginner's Sales Strategy

Seed cotton formula	One-tier: Initial price only	Two-tier: low initial price & bonus linked to ginner performance	Two-tier: low initial price & bonus linked to market average	One-tier: Final price only
Main ginner's sales strategy to minimize price risk exposure.	Sell forward fixed as soon as volume and quality known: ■ Should lock-in margin at initial price negotiation ahead of season, i.e. sell forward fixed. ■ Exact volumes and qualities only known gradually over season.	Sell forward partially ahead to secure initial price, then do best to beat breakeven over the season and optimize return (ginner is in a joint venture with producers)	Sell forward partially ahead to secure initial price, then replicate passively market average to limit exposure to bonus.	Exposure borne by producers; ginner acts mostly as intermediary, selling back to market upon seed cotton purchase/agreement on final price.

is that Benin's atomized private ginners have a much weaker sales management capacity and performance than the large public-private partnership Sofitex in Burkina Faso, whose manager enjoys an excellent reputation.

When designing a privatization scheme, it is crucial to target the proper investors. The technical specifications should clearly require investors with: a) a substantial track record in cotton price risk management, b) willingness and ability to have a ginning operation with a critical size that ensures a lasting commitment to the financial viability of the local franchise, within the context of the international operator's global position management.[43] Another decision is whether to include the producers as minority shareholders in the ginneries. This has been relatively successful in Burkina Faso and has the advantage of reducing potential conflicts of interest such as between the ginner's need to reduce costs and his need to build a trust-based and transparent relationship with producers who will then be motivated to continue to grow cotton.

Building the MIS tools and institutional capacity of public or local private ginners is a more useful target for Government financial support than covering sector deficits that could be artificially inflated or caused by endogenous inefficiencies. In case the ginners in the market do not have the analytical tools and expertise described in the above-section,

---

43. Concretely, this means for example the need to ensure that the investor does pursue the objective of optimal sales revenues of the local ginning undertaking, i.e. does not display artificially low sales prices to transfer profits to its global commodities trading unit,

that could be a field worthy of government's financial support, provided the operator can prove his capacity and willingness to provide long term continuity to the knowledge transferred. This includes adequate analytical accounting, position management instruments, counterpart exposures tracking and contract enforcements, personnel training at the best cotton schools, and facilitating the adoption of web-based auctions for part of the production.

Governments, donors and ginners should interact regularly with the main international exchanges to put on their agenda the possibility to create a world cotton futures contract. The current absence of an organized exchange offering futures contracts on non-U.S. cottons is a serious obstacle to effective price risk hedging by ginners in WCA. The most recent attempt by Euronext was very nearly successful, and such initiatives should be revived. Whether it ends up being quoted on the Zenghzou, NYCE or Euronext, a World Cotton Future contract that allows for physical delivery of WCA cotton origins, among others, would be a significant achievement. As the share of non-U.S. cotton volumes in exported cotton grows, the need for such a contract will only become more pressing over time, especially if the United States lifts its subsidies resulting in a decrease in U.S. cotton production. The growing volumes of non-U.S. cotton should allow for an adequate liquidity of such a futures contract, especially if its launch is widely disseminated to the trading, ginning, spinning and hedge funds communities.

CHAPTER 5

Promoting Competitiveness Through Sector Reforms

John Baffes and Ilhem Baghdadli

The need to enhance private participation in the management of the cotton sector in WCA is clear. With fungible resources, States do not have enough budget to make the investments needed to achieve the best possible improvements in farms yields and cost reduction as well as to increase and smoothen cotton sales revenues. Yet, these improvements are most needed in the Cotton-4 countries, where cotton is a major contributor to export revenues and economic growth. Privatization is meant at improving competitiveness and, therefore, is a tool to enhance market efficiency and ultimately welfare.

Lessons learned from the 1990s suggest that transferring public property to private enterprises is not enough, by itself, to put the sector back to a sustainable path. Policy reforms in cotton sectors should not only consist of making the decision to privatize, they should provide guidance on how to privatize by articulating the three steps of a sound privatization scheme.

- Restructure the market by identifying what market structure should replace the vertically integrated monopoly
- Deregulate the industry by articulating how to go from public monopoly to the new market setting (strengthen competition law and build contracting devices and capacities, while removing regulations)
- Actually transfer some or all the property rights of the monopoly to the private sector.

It is extremely important to keep in mind that economic policy is often an outcome of trial and error process rather than a science. Therefore, lessons learned from past experiences are key in the search for improvement. However, such lessons are not always replicable. Each market setting reflects primarily past decisions which, in turn, determines the span of feasible options. Lessons that can be useful at the beginning of a process may not be useful later on.

This chapter argues that Industrial Organization criteria could be effective tools in the design of future privatization. The findings are not meant to apply to countries, which have already implemented a privatization scheme.

Re-structuring Markets

Point of Departure and the Likely Market Structures

When considering privatization, the first concern relates to the identification of what market structure should replace the vertically integrated monopoly. Evidence indicates that private monopoly can be even worse than public monopoly in terms of market efficiency and welfare distribution. It is thus very important to restructure the market appropriately before transferring the assets to the private investors. Whether segments (ginning, transport, research and extension, input provision) are bundled together or sold separately have important implications on the sale's value as well as on the efficiency of the new market structure.

Re-structuring markets should entail privatization process that improves market efficiency and welfare in a sustainable way. The market structure that attracts the highest bid is not necessarily consistent with long term welfare. What matters the most is the types of improvement that take place in the sector along with the sustainability of the sector's growth.

Sound restructuring requires not only identifying the point of departure, which for many cotton producing countries is (or was) a vertically integrated monopoly, but also

Figure 14. Market Structures for Cotton Chain Supply

RESTRAINTS		HORIZONTAL		
		HIGH	.....	LOW
VERTICAL	HIGH	**A** One integrated monopoly handles all transactions in the chain, such as ginning, transport, input supply.	....	**B** The integrated monopoly is separated according to horizontally-related activities (an example is regional zoning.)
	....	....		....
	LOW	**C** The integrated monopoly is separated according to vertically-related functions or activities.	....	**D** Atomized market structure Theoretical benchmark

specifying the ultimate market structure. For a summary illustration of the likely market structures consider figure 10 which depicts the likely polar market structures within a 2×2 matrix. It should be emphasized that figure 10 represents a continuum with cells A, B, C and D representing extreme cases. In reality, actual market structures are likely to be in between as depicted by the shaded areas.

The upper-left cell of the matrix, A, represents the integrated monopoly, a typical structure in some WCA (and other SSA countries prior to reforms). Some of the key characteristics are:

- The monopoly handles all transactions in the chain, such as ginning, transport, input supply.
- The monopoly is owned by the state, which set the rule of most transaction (such as pan-territorial and pan-seasonal prices).
- Farmers are obliged to sell their cotton to the company (either individually or through cooperatives).
- Ginners are obliged to buy cotton at a set price regardless of the margin cost of production (in effect, such this structure transfers resources from efficient to inefficient producers).

At the other extreme, the lower-right cell, D, represents the pure and perfect market structure, which is a theoretical benchmark with the following key features:

- Atomized market structure.
- All firms are private are profit maximizers.
- No barrier to entry or to exit the market.

In the high-vertical, low-horizontal restraint case, B, the monopoly is broken into regional monopolies, as is the case in Burkina Faso. The key characteristics of this setting are the following:

- Each firm operate within an exclusive territory.
- The vertical structure of the sector is retained within each territory—each company operates its own ginneries, supplies inputs, and so forth.
- Within a territory there might be several ginners. When this is the case, cotton growers may have the choice to sell to any ginner within the territory, but are not allowed to sell outside the zone.

The low-vertical, high-horizontal restraint case, C, the integrated monopoly is separated according to functions of the supply chain. The key features are as follows:

- Each firm operates with exclusive monopoly rights on one activity (ginning, input supply, transportation, and extension)
- There is more integration of vertical activities (i.e.: different companies handles the activities)
- Each activity is performed by a monopoly or a many companies, which form a cartel.

While it is clear that the integrated monopoly and perfect competition are not feasible alternatives, the former because of poor past performance and the latter because of the market failures, the choice between the remaining two cases is less clear. Unfortunately, in most occasions, these two restructuring processes have not been clearly articulated in the reforms process.

Criteria to Assess Likely Market Structures

There are competition rules, which are meant to govern any market in almost any part of the world, and these rules should be used as a guideline to design competitive market structures in the cotton sector in WCA.

Competition rules were first introduced by Senator Sherman, who ordered the break-down of the Standard Oil company (then owned by Rockefeller) into 35 vertically integrated oil companies, in 1890. The Sherman Act included a section on the prohibition of trusts and a section outlawing monopolization or any attempt to monopolize markets. A tremendous amount of jurisprudential cases have been developed based on these two rulings, which remain the pillars of the American competition rules.

Considerable amount of economic research, classified in Industrial organization and antitrust Law, was used to back up the Senator's decision to break down the Rockefeller Empire and even more research was developed then after to help Judges assess market structures and their effects on efficiency and welfare. Among the most seminal contributions (some of them are Nobel Price recipients): "New Developments on the Oligopoly Front" by Franco Modigliani (1958), "The Theory of Oligopoly" by George Stigler (1964); "Diagnosing Monopoly" by Franklin Fisher (1979); "An Essay on the Economics of Imperfect Information" by Michael Rothschild and Joseph Stiglitz (1986); "Moral Hazard in Teams" by Bengt Holmstrom (1982); "Theory of Vertical and Lateral Integration" by Sanford Grossman and Oliver Hart (1986); "On the Theory of Perfectly-contestable Markets" by Baumol, Panzar, and Willing (1986).

The European Treaty includes competition rules, which are similar to the American competition devices. Indeed, Article 81 of the European Treaty (for long known as being Article 85 of the Rome treaty) bans trusts and Article 82 (ex-Article 86) prohibits any abuse of dominant position (rather than monopolization and any attempts of monopolization as is the case in the American competition rules). While the underlying principles of the American competition rules and the European competition rules are the same, the latest acknowledges the existence of market failures and the need for some sort of coordination between firms. Major developments in Competition Law concerned vertical restraints such as exclusive dealing, franchising and selective distribution, which are now included in the Block Exemption.[44]

---

44. As defined in the Glossary of Terms used in EU competition policy, the Block Exemption is a 'regulation issued by the Commission or by the Council pursuant to Article 81(3) of the EC Treaty, specifying the conditions under which certain types of agreements are exempted from prohibition on restrictive agreements laid down in Article 81(1) of the EC Treaty. When an agreement fulfils the conditions set out in a block exemption regulation, individual notification of that agreement is not necessary: the agreement is automatically valid and enforceable. Block exemption regulation exist, for instance, for vertical agreements, Research and Development agreements, specialization agreements, and technology transfer agreements.

While the WAEMU competition Law is not enforced in a number of sectors such as cotton, it exists and is are very much in line with European Competition law, which is based on the very principle of the Sherman Act and the assumption that market failures prevents pure and perfect competition. Indeed, regulation N° 03/2002/CM/UEMOA prohibits trust and the abuse of a dominant position.

To issue their ruling, Judges have build considerable knowledge on many issues such as market foreclosure, intra-brand and inter-brand competition, exclusive territories and retail price maintenance. We believe that this knowledge should no longer be ignored when designing market structures in WCA cotton sectors.

In the framework of the existing competition rules, the comparisons of various market structures can be based on the following four criteria: Economies of scale, economies of scope, improved connectivity between market segments, and hold-up risk.

- Economies of scale may justify uniting (horizontally-related) market segments, if enlarging the scale of operations enhances the cost structure. For example, reducing the number of ginneries from 6 to 4 is worth considering if having 4 ginneries is more effective. While this criterion, along with the others, can only be tested on a case-by-case basis, it suggests that having many operators to perform a particular activity may not be the best way to promote market competitiveness. In light of market failures, sound competition is not predicated on a large number of operators, but rather an optimal number.
- Economies of scope may justify uniting (horizontally or vertically-related) market segments if enlarging a firm's range of activities (e.g. sharing infrastructure or equipment) results in cost savings. For instance, having the same operator handles both ginning and oil crushing may merit consideration if these two activities, one combined, reduce costs.
- Improved connectivity between market segments may justify joining them, if it enables saving on coordination costs. For instance, input distribution and lint transportation are connected to the demand for transport services in the same ways. Therefore joining these two activities may save cost.
- Hold-up risk occurs when the possibility that a firm benefits from the actions and efforts of another without paying for or sharing the costs preclude the transaction. This risk is higher when: (i) investment are specific; (ii) the transaction might not be frequent and durable, (iii) the level of uncertainty surrounding the relation is important; (iv) measuring the performance of one of the contractors is complex; (v) the transaction is not connected to others.

While almost no deal can be done without investment, all investments are not of the same type. Certain specific investments should not be undertaken if there is a probability the transaction is not carried out. For example, if a contracting firm may break his commitment in a deal involving investments in specific assets there might be no supplier willing to undertake the contract. Here, an efficient way to ensure the existence of the market—a corollary to the deal—is merging the actors' interests. The incentive to merge may be even greater when the contractors have to interact frequently and/or over the long term. It may also be greater when the circumstances surrounding or determining the deal are highly uncertain, and when measuring the performance of a co-contractor is too difficult. (The risk associated with these factors determining the level of hold-up risk).

The following section explains how these criteria may plead in favor of market structures which are between the polar cases B and D of our matrix.

The Need for Vertical Coordination

Vertical structuring is not subject to the same rules as horizontal structuring, since vertical restraints are generally seen as less harmful to competition than horizontal ones. West African competition law (WAEMU) is very much in line with European Competition law (EC), which clearly acknowledges market imperfections and the opportunity for stakeholders to benefit from them.

The need for vertical coordination may prevent separation of activities, when hold-up risks are high and contracting devices and capacities are insufficient. Cotton supply chains encompass numerous risks:

- Research & extension services are not offered properly and adequately, thus having a negative effect on yields and production.
- Input supplies are offered at high prices, often of inappropriate quality and not the right delivery timeframe.
- Transport is characterized by high costs because of volume fragmentation; often they are no timely.
- Trading of lint is often characterized by mismanagement of cotton price volatility.

During the process of developing private capacities, some activities can be handled under the earlier market structure (for example, *transport services* and *input distribution* may continue to be handled by the *ginning business*). For ginners, medium-term contracts are perhaps the best way to manage the hold-up risks inherent to the provision of transport services and input supply. However, in WCA, the private sector does not have the capacity to provide quality services in a timely fashion—in either transport or input distribution. Thus, taking input supply and transport out of the ginners' control may jeopardize the cotton supply chain. The best solution available to the sector might be for the ginner to use his own fleet of transporters to mitigate the risks to his business of relying on private transporters. The same arguments apply to input distribution.

If there are private capacities for performing an activity, then the earlier monopoly should not be allowed to have privileged command on it (e.g. there are over fifteen traders active in WCA, thus *trading* should not continue to be handle the *ginning* buisiness). Ginners must have the skills and capacity needed to understand the deals they are committed to, but they do not need to have a trading unit or use long-term contracts to win traders' loyalty.

The nature of *research and extension services* must be clearly established before restructuring the cotton supply chain. If research and extension is a public good (which is often the viewed as being the case), it should not be under the ginners control. The terms and conditions for these activities should be formalized in law or a contract. If it is not to be a public good, it should remain within the ginners domain since this is the actor in the supply chain with the greatest financial capacity. Moreover, ginners are the most highly invested in the quality of research and extension services as their sales revenues are positively correlated to it. An alternative to the ginner handling Research and extension could be contracting it out.

Producers and *ginners* can use contracts to manage the risks underlying the production of seed cotton and its timely collection. High transport costs together with the specific investments that cotton producers have to make may justify exclusive deals between a ginner and producers. WCA producers have in some occasion been given the opportunity to buy shares in a ginnery and thereby allying their interests with those of the ginner. As producers don't have tremendous financial means, which implies that the share they are offered is small, the process can generate benefits through synergies between production and ginning.

What Types of Investors are Needed?

The main challenge ahead for the Cotton-4 lies in improving the competitiveness of the cotton supply chain. Yet, achieving this will require more than just financial assistance. The cotton sectors in these countries need access to the best available tools and additional capacity-building. Poorly designed sales strategies can, in fact, undermine all efforts to increase yields, improve costs structures and enhance grading. Increasing yields requires investment in research and extension services, but tapping into the specific know-how of international market players may be even more important. These players can assist in the design of technical packages and help identify incentives for farmers to adhere more closely to technical recommendations. While restructuring the cotton supply chain can significantly improve the industry's cost structure, improved technologies and better equipment are also needed. As international strategic investors make international arbitrage and only enters the markets which are the most profitable, cost benefit analysis must be developed to establish whether the improvements they might bring into the market are worth the cost to pay to have them in. Consortium involving international and local investors might be the most effective way to access international best practice at a reasonable cost.

Given the fact that some activities should not be separated from the outset, privatization schemes should target potential investors that bring, in addition to cash, better management, privileged access to the best available know-how, technologies and equipment. In Burkina Faso, for instance, the government targeted two types of investors: producers and international strategic investors (Dagris and Reinhart). Producers were identified as the investors who could bring the best synergies between seed cotton production and ginning in regional vertically-integrated monopolies. International strategic investors were identified as the investors who could bring to the supply chain, not only cash, but also know-how, new techniques of management, and improved equipment. In Benin, on the other hand, the government targeted only local investors, who were charged with taking over various activities along the cotton supply chain. These types of investors were expected to charge less than international strategic investors for quality services.

Articulating the Main Steps of the De-regulation Process before Transferring Public Property to Private Investors

To promote competitiveness, cotton sector reform must be consistent with (i) restructuring the cotton supply chain into appropriate lots in order to maximize the performance of the

---

Box 9: Assessment of Vertical Restraints

Imposition of vertical restraints is typically associated with numerous negative effects on the sector in question. The guidelines on vertical restraints issued by the European Commission, for example, list four such limitations: (i) foreclosure of other suppliers or other buyers by raising barriers to entry; (ii) less brand competition among the companies operating on a market; (iii) less brand competition among distributors; and (iv) limitations on consumer freedom to purchase goods or services in a Member State. Although not all these limitation may be applicable to the cotton sector, their explicit recognition by the EC guidelines can become a useful tool when designing deregulation and privatization.

However, vertical restraints often have positive effects and may be justifiable for a limited period where:

■   one distributor is "free-riding" on the promotion efforts of another distributor;

■   a manufacturer wants to enter a new geographic market, for instance, by exporting to another country for the first time. This may involve certain "first-time investments" by the distributor to establish the brand in the market;

■   certain retailers in some sectors have a reputation for stocking only "quality" products;

■   client-specific investments have to be made by either the supplier or the buyer, such as in special equipment or training;

■   know-how, once provided, cannot be taken back, and the provider of the know-how may not want it to be used on behalf of, or by, his competitors;

■   in order to exploit economies of scale and thereby lower his product's retail price, the manufacturer may want to concentrate the resale of his product among a limited number of distributors;

■   the usual providers of capital (banks, equity markets) provide capital sub-optimally when they have imperfect information on the quality of the borrower or the basis for securing the loan is inadequate; and

■   a manufacturer increases sales by imposing a certain measure of uniformity and standard of quality on his distributors. This may enable him to create a brand image and thereby attract consumers. This can be found, for instance, in exclusive dealing, selective distribution and franchising.

Source: Guidelines on vertical restraints, European Commission.

targeted investors; (ii) strengthening competition law and building contracting devices and capacities, while removing regulations and (iii) designing sound privatization by targeting investors that, in addition to maximizing the price they are willing to pay, they ensure competitiveness.

Structuring markets is crucial to enhancing performances. Evidence has shown that different market structures perform differently in terms of efficiency and subsequent market values of the lots to be privatized. The cotton supply chain is characterized by a need for vertical coordination, because of high hold-up risks and non existing contracting devices to effectively manage such risks. On the other hand, horizontal agreements are not subject to the same problem, since such they might be more harmful to competition. Very much inspired by the European model, the competition policy enforced in the WAEMU zone forbids abuse of a dominant position. Minimizing the risk of this abuse suggests that monopolies need to be restructured into, at least, four entities. But this number is a theoretical benchmark and the number of companies leading to optimal market performance depends on returns on scale/scope and other market failures. These factors can only be analyzed on a case-by-case basis.

Deregulating the integrated monopoly would require building competition rules, contracting devices and capacities that eventually will lead to a successful privatization. For instance, Governments should elaborate on the seed cotton pricing schemes well before the sale. This will enable investors to soundly evaluate their potential returns and bid accordingly. If seed cotton pricing schemes are unclear, this will be reflected in the bids. Laws governing competition, contracting devices and capacity must all be developed and in place before deregulation and the transfer of public property to private enterprise. Government should also adhere to and publicize realistic timeframes for the completion of the privatization process.

Governments must have clear and reasonable expectations regarding privatization, and a strong commitment to its implementation. If the Government wants to attract international strategic investors, able to provide not only cash, but privileged market access, new technology and management expertise, it must assure investors that it will not use its political power, residual shares, or golden share in a way that jeopardizes the company's ability to maximize profits and efficiency. Transparency, which is crucial to avoiding corruption and controversy, can be fostered by publicity campaigns and the use of third-party financial advisers, who can carry out asset valuations to ensure that prices are realistic, fair and consistent, as well institute procedures for soliciting bids and evaluating offers. At any rate, governments must provide investors with clear information on the value of the assets at stake. In order to present investors with reliable data on the assets and liabilities for sale, in a comprehensible format, governments need to hire an international accounting firm to perform an end-of-year audit and prepare consolidated financial statements of the businesses in question, in accordance with international accounting standards.

Appendixes

Implications of Cotton Policies

Numerous models have evaluated the impact of cotton policies on the cotton market with considerable variation in the results. The International Cotton Advisory Committee, for example, concluded that in the absence of direct subsidies, average cotton prices during the 2000/01 season would have been 30 percent higher than what they actually were (ICAC 2002). The study, which was based on a short run partial equilibrium model, did acknowledge that while removal of subsidies would result in lower production in the countries which receive them (and hence higher prices in the short term), such impact would be partially offset by shifting production to non-subsidizing countries in the medium to longer terms. Goreux (2004), who extended the ICAC model by replacing the base year with 1998–2002 average subsidies, estimated that in the absence of support the world price of cotton would have been between 3 and 13 percent higher in these five years, depending on the value of demand and supply elasticities. Gillson and others (2004) using subsidy data for 1999 and a model similar to that of Goreux (2004), estimated that removal of subsidies by the United States, EU, and China would increase the world price of cotton by 18 percent.

Reeves and others (2001) and others used a Computable General Equilibrium model and found that removal of production and export subsidies by the United States and the EU will induce a 20 percent reduction in U.S. cotton production, a 50 percent reduction in U.S. cotton exports, with much higher figures for the EU. They also estimated that if support was not in place, world cotton prices would be 10.7 percent higher compared to their 2001/02 levels. Simulations from a model developed by the Food and Agriculture Policy Research Institute (FAPRI 2002) found that under global liberalization (removal of trade barriers and domestic support of all commodity sectors including cotton), the world cotton price would increase over the baseline scenario by an average of 12.7 percent over a 10-year period. Based largely on FAPRI's data and assumptions, Sumner (2003) estimated that had all U.S. cotton subsidies not been in place during the marketing years 1999–2002, the world price of cotton would have been almost 13 percent higher (see Figure 2 for nominal cotton prices during the past two decades).

Based on a partial equilibrium model, Tokarick (2003) finds that multilateral trade liberalization in all agricultural markets (including cotton) would induce a 2.8 percent increase in the world price of cotton and a $95 million annual increase in welfare. Poonyth and others (2004) and others estimate that removal of cotton subsidies—as reported in the WTO notifications—would increase the world price of cotton between 3.1 percent and 4.8 percent, depending on assumptions about demand and supply elasticities. In contrast, Shepherd (2004) and Pan and others (2004) and others find a negligible impact of subsidies on the world price of cotton.

The highly divergent results for these models reflect in part the structure of the models and the assumed elasticities. Several other factors also influence the results. The reasons behind the highly divergent results of cotton models were the subject of an FAO experts' consultation (FAO 2004). First, there are differences in the level and structure of support. For example, some models incorporate China's support to its cotton sector and model its removal; others do not. Second, there are differences in the underlying scenarios. Some models assume liberalization in all commodity markets while others assume liberalization only in the cotton sector. Third, the models use different base years and hence different levels of subsidies. For example, support in the United States was three times as high in 1999 as in 1997. Setting all the differences aside, however a simple average over all models shows that world cotton prices would have been about 10 percent higher without support. Applying a simple average to the Francophone Africa cotton producing countries shows that these countries lost approximately $150 million annually in export earnings due to the subsidies.

Not all models report results on the gainers and losers from the removal of cotton subsidies. In that respect the most complete analysis is offered by the FAPRI model, which finds the largest gains in trade for Africa, with an expected average increase in exports of 12.6 percent. Exports increase by 6.0 percent for Uzbekistan and by 2.7 percent for Australia, while exports from the United States decline by 3.5 percent. The most dramatic impact is on the production side. The European Union's cotton output would decline by more than 70 percent—not a complete surprise considering that the European Union's cotton output during the late 1990s was three times higher than it was before Greece and Spain joined.

Cotton and the Sixth WTO Ministerial in Hong Kong

Cotton received considerable attention during the sixth WTO ministerial in Hong Kong. Widespread fears that the cotton initiative may contribute to another Cancun-type failure did not materialize. Consistent with the convention established at the Cotonou workshop (March 23–24, 2004), the text of the declaration deals separately with the issue of trade (paragraph 110) and development (paragraph 12).

On export subsides, the declaration says that "all forms of export subsidies for cotton will be eliminated by developed countries in 2006." Because the EU does not give any export subsidies, the text is relevant only to the United States. The two types of U.S. export subsidies given are (i) the export credit guarantees and (ii) the Step-2 payment, both of which must be discontinued according to the WTO's Panel findings (case DS267). Furthermore, given that the USTR office publicly announced that it will fully comply with the Panel's ruling (to be approved by the U.S. Congress), the declaration on export subsidies adds no new commitment. Note that export subsidies represented about 12 percent of total cotton support during 1995–2002.

On market access, the declaration says that "developed countries will give duty and quota free access for cotton for cotton exports from least-developed countries from the commencement of the implementation period." Again, this text is relevant only to the United States because the EU does not impose any border restriction on cotton imports—it would have been relevant to China if it were considered a developed country by the WTO. Although the United States applies TRQs on cotton imports, because it is (and has been always) a net cotton exporter, the TRQs are largely irrelevant. Any increase in U.S. cotton imports due to the removal of TRQs, is likely to cause trade diversion rather than trade generation. For example, some U.S. textiles may use imported instead of domestically produced cotton while the U.S. cotton they would have used will be exported. Again, as was the case with export subsidies, the market access part of the declaration is unlikely to make any material difference.

Finally, on domestic support, the declaration says that ". . . trade distorting subsidies for cotton production should be reduced more ambitiously than under whatever general formula is agreed and that it should be implemented over a shorter period of time than generally applicable." A number of issues are relevant to this part of the declaration. The EU has already reformed its cotton program, the three key elements of which are: (i) 65%/35% decoupled/area payments; (ii) €700 million cap per annum; (iii) duration until 2013. Thus, it appears than none of these elements are likely to change as a result of the declaration. Therefore, the domestic support part of the declaration (as was the case with the other two pillars) is applicable to the United States only.

The first issue relates to the definition of trade distorting subsidies; while the United States has placed direct payments (and the earlier production flexibility contracts) in the green box, the WTO Panel ruled that they should have been placed in the amber box because of the prohibition of planting fruits and vegetables on the eligible land. If direct payments are placed in the amber box, then, with the exception of crop insurance (which represents only a small fraction of the budgetary outlays), the entire cotton program should be placed in the amber box; thus, any ambitious reduction has to be calculated over the full expenditures.

However, regardless of where direct payments are placed, the United States should not have exceeded the 1992 level of support. During the 1992 marketing year, the United States disbursed $2.01 billion to its cotton sector. The average disbursements during dispute years (1999–2002) were $3.22 billion (these are the figures are consistent with the ones used by the Panel). Therefore, taking as a base the market conditions and subsidy levels experienced during 1999–2002, the United States must undertake an almost 40 percent reduction just to comply with the Panel's ruling. To that, if one adds the commitments to be agreed under the general reduction formula to be agreed on domestic support as well as any additional cuts due to "ambitiousness", one should expect a substantial reduction of U.S. cotton subsidies. To what extent this will be the case depends, among other factors, on the 2007 Farm Bill, discussions of which will begin soon.

Bibliography

Amprou, Jacky. 2005. "Crise Ivoirienne et Flux Régionaux de Transport." AFD. Processed.

Araujo-Bonjean, Catherine, Jean-Louis Combes, and Patrick Plane. 2003. "Preserving Vertical Co-ordination in the West African Cotton Sector." Document de travail de la série Etudes et Documents E 2003.03, CERDI, CNRS-Université d'Auvergne.

Bateman, Milford. 1998. "Local Supply Chain Development in the Transition Economies: The Case of Kazakhstan." *Supply Chain Management* 3(2):79–88.

Badiane, Ousmane, Dhaneshwar Ghura, Louis Goreux, and Paul Masson. 2002. "Cotton Sector Strategies in West and Central Africa." World Bank Policy Research Working Paper 2867, Washington, D.C.

Baffes, John. 2005. "The 'Cotton Problem.'" *The World Bank Research Observer* 20(1):109–44.

Baumol, W., J. Panzar, and R. Willing. 1986. "On the theory of perfectly-contestable markets." In J. Stiglitz and F. Mathewson, eds. *New Development in the Analysis of Market Structure*. Cambridge, Mass.: Macmillan.

Bourdet, Yves. 2004. "A Tale of Three Countries." Country Economic Report 2004:2. SIDA.

Csaki, Csaba. 2000. "Agricultural Reforms in Central and Eastern Europe and the Former Soviet Union—Status and Perspectives." *Agricultural Economics* 9(3):37–54.

Fisher, Franklin. 1979. "Diagnosing Monopoly." *Quarterly Review of Economic and Business* 19:7–33.

Fock, Michel. 1998a. "Cotton Yield Stagnation: Addressing a Common Effect of Various Causes." In the proceedings of the World Cotton Research Conference 2, Athens 5–11.

———. 1998b. "Le Développement du Coton au Mali par Analyse des Contradictions: les Acteurs et les Crises de 1985 à 1993." *Document de travail de l'UR Economie des Filières*, Cirad.

Freud, Claude. 1999. "Politiques des Prix et Performances des Filières Cotonnières en Afrique." *Revue Tiers Monde* 160:929–43.

GDS. 2004. "Value Chain Analysis of Selected Strategic Sectors in Kenya." Processed.

Gaborel, Christian, Houngnibo. 2005. "Origine des Recommandations sur la Fertilisation du Secteur Cotonnier en Afrique de l'Ouest. Etat des Lieux et Quel Futur?" *Document de travail IFDC*.

Gereffi, Gary. 1994. "The Organization of Buyer-Driven Global Commodity Chains: How U.S. Retailers Shape Overseas Production Networks." In Gary Gereffi and Miguel Korzeniewicz, *Commodity Chains and Global Capitalism*. Westport, Conn.: Praeger.

Gergely, Nicolas. 2004. "Etude Comparative sur les Coûts de Production des Sociétés Cotonnières au Mali, au Burkina Faso et au Cameroun." Rapport pour l'Agence Française de Développement.

Gibbon, Peter. 1999. "Free Competition Without Sustainable Development? Cotton Sector Liberalization, 1994/95 to 1997/98." *Journal of Development Studies* 36(1):128–50.

Gillson, I., C. Poulton, K. Balcombe, and S. Page. 2004. "Understanding the Impact of Cotton Subsidies on Developing Countries and Poor People in those Countries." Working paper, Overseas Development Institute, London.

Goletti, Francesco, and Philippe Chabot. 2000. "Food Policy Research for Improving the Reform of Agricultural Input and Output Markets in Central Asia." *Food Policy* 25:661–79.

Goreux, Louis, and John Macrae. 2003. "Reforming the Cotton Sector in Sub-Saharan Africa." *Africa Region Working Paper 47.*

Guchgeldiev, Oleg. 1999. "Comprehensive Economic Study of Cotton Production Sub-Sector in Turkmenistan." Masters Degree dissertation, University of Birmingham.

Grossman, Sanford, and Oliver Hart. 1986. "The Costs and Benefits of Ownership: A Theory of Vertical and Lateral Integration." *Journal of Political Economy* 94(4):691–719.

Holmstrom, Bengt. 1982. "Moral Hazard in Teams." *Bell Journal of Economics* 13(2):324–40.

Hopkins, Terence, and Immanuel Wallerstein. 1986. "Commodity Chains in the World Economy Prior to 1800." *Review* 10(1)157–70.

Hugon, Philippe. 2005. "Les Filières Cotonnières Africaines au Regard de l'Economie du Développement." Processed.

Hugon, Philippe, and Abel Mayeyenda. 2003. "Les Effets des Politiques des Prix dans les Filières Coton en Afrique Zone Franc: Analyse Empirique." *Economie rurale* 275: 66–82.

ICAC. 2002. *Production and Trade Policy Affecting the Cotton Industry.* Washington, D.C.

IFDC. 2005a. "L'Etat du Marché des Intrants Agricoles au Bénin." Muscle Shoals (AL).

———. 2005b "Structure du prix des engrais en Afrique de l'Ouest." Processed.

Kim, Alexander. 2005. "Abandoned by the State: Cotton Production in South Kyrgyzstan." Paper presented at the SOAS conference Cotton Sector in Central Asia: Economic Policy and Development Challenges, London, November 3–4.

Leibenstein, H. 1966. "Allocative Efficiency vs. X-efficiency." *American Economic Review* 58(June).

Lerman, Zvi, Csaba Csaki, and Gershon Feder. 2004. *Agriculture in Transition.* Lanham, Md.: Lexington Books.

Micarelli, M. 1991. "International Markets and Perspectives for Central American Traditional Exports: Coffee, Cotton and Bananas." In Wim Pelupessy, *Perspectives on the Agro-export Economy in Central America.* Pittsburgh, Penn.: University of Pittsburgh Press.

Modigliani, Franco. 1958. "New developments on the Oligopoly front." *Journal of Political Economy* 66(June):215–32.

National Commission of Competition and Consumption in Burkina Faso. 2000. *Status Report on Competition and Consumption in Burkina Faso.*

ONUDI. 2004. "Identification d'un Plan d'Action d'Amélioration de la Qualité et de la Valorisation de la Qualité du Coton dans les pays de l'UEMOA." Processed.

Pan, S., S. Mohanty, D. Ethridge, and M. Fadiga. 2004. "The Impacts of U.S. Cotton Programs on the World Market: An Analysis of Brazilian and West African WTO Petitions." Department of Agricultural and Applied Economics, Texas Tech University.

Pastor, Gonzalo, and Ron Van Rooden. 2004. "Turkmenistan—the Burden of Current Agricultural Policies." *Emerging Markets, Finance and Trade* 40(1):35–58.

Pomfret, Richard. 2006. *The Central Asian Economies since Independence.* Princeton, N.J.: Princeton University Press.

Poonyth, D., A. Sarris, R. Sharma, and S. Shui. 2004. "The Impact of Domestic and Trade Policies on the World Cotton Market." Commodity and Trade Policy Research Working Paper, Food and Agriculture Organization, Rome.

Poulton, Colin, Peter Gibbon, Benjamine Hanyani-Mlambo, Jonathan Hydd, Wilbald Maro, Marianne Nylandsted Larsen, Afonso Osorio, and David Tschirley. 2004. "Competition and Coordination in Liberalized African Cotton Market Systems." *World Development Report* 32(3):519–36.

Pursell, G., and M. Diop. 1998. "Cotton Policies in Francophone Africa." The World Bank, Washington, D.C., Processed.

Raballand, Gaël, Antoine Kunth, and Richard Auty. 2005. "Central Asia's Transport Cost Burden and Its Impact on Trade." *Economic Systems* 29(1):6–31.

Raikes, Philip, Michael Friis Frensen, and Stefano Ponte. 2000. "Global Commodity Chain Analysis and the French *Filière* Approach: Comparison and Critique." *Economy and Society* 29(3):390–417.

Reeves, G., D. Vincent, D. Quirke, and S. Wyatt. 2001. "Trade Distortions and Cotton Markets: Implications for Global Cotton Producers." Canberra, Australia: Center for International Economics.

République du Tchad, Ministère du Plan, du Développement et de la Coopération. 2004. *Rapport de Présentation du Deuxième Lot de Scenarii de Privatisation.*

Rothschild, Michael, and Joseph Stiglitz. 1986. "An Essay on the Economics of Imperfect Information." *Quarterly Journal of Economics* 90(4):629–49.

Sadler, Marc. 2005. "Vertical Coordination in the Cotton Supply Chains in Central Asia." In Jo Swinnen, ed., *Supply Chains in Transition.* Forthcoming.

Sarris, Alexander. 2000. "Has world cereal market instability increased?" *Food Policy* 25(2):337–50.

Shankar, Bhavani, and Colin Thirtle. 2004. "Pesticide Productivity and Transgenic Cotton Technology: The South African Smallholder Case." *Journal of Agricultural Economics* 56(1):97–116.

Shepherd, B. 2004. "The Impact of U.S. Subsidies on the World Market of Cotton: A Reassessment." Groupe d'Economie Mondiale (GEM), Institut d'Etudes Politiques de Paris.

SOFRECO. 2000. "Audit Technique Industriel et Commercial de la CMD—Audit de la Fonction Transport."

Souley, Halimatou. 2001. "Déréglementation du Transport Routier de Marchandises au Niger et Intégration Sous-Régionale." Thèse de l'Université de Paris Val de Marne.

Spoor, Max. 2003. "Agrarian Reform in Post-Soviet States Revisited: Central Asia and Mongolia." In Max Spoor, *Transition, Institutions, and the Rural Sector.* Lanham, Md.: Lexington Books.

Stigler, George. 1964. "The Theory of Oligopoly." *Journal of Political Economy* 72 (February):44–61.

Tokarick, S. 2003. "Measuring the Impact of Distortions in Agricultural Trade in Partial and General Equilibrium." International Monetary Fund Working Paper WP/03/110, Washington, D.C.

Townsend, Terry, and Andrei Guitchounts. 1994. "A Survey of Cotton Income and Price Support Programs." In proceedings of the Beltwide Cotton: A Proposal for WTO Negotiation. *World Trade Review* 2(1):5–31.

Trevisani, Tommaso. 2005. "The Emerging Actor of the Decollectivization in Uzbekistan: Private Farming between Newly Defined Political Constraints and Opportunities." Paper presented at the SOAS conference Cotton Sector in Central Asia: Economic Policy and Development Challenges, London, November 3–4.

UMEOA. 2003. "Rapport d'Analyse des Résultats de l'Enquête des Chauffeurs." Processed.

Valdes, Alberto, and William Foster. 2003. "Special Safeguards for Developing Countries: A Proposal for WTO Negotiation." *World Trade Review* 2(1):5–31.

Welch, Dick, and Olivier Fremond. 1998. *The Case-by-Case Approach to Privatization. Techniques and Examples.* World Bank Technical Paper No. 403. Washington, D.C.: The World Bank.

World Bank. 2005a. "Chad—Diagnostic Trade Integration Study." Draft.

———. 2005b. "Kyrgyz Republic—Country Economic Memorandum." Draft.

———. 2005c. "Stratégie de Facilitation du Transport et Transit pour Stimuler la Croissance au Mali." Processed.

Eco-Audit

Environmental Benefits Statement

The World Bank is committed to preserving Endangered Forests and natural resources. We print World Bank Working Papers and Country Studies on 100 percent postconsumer recycled paper, processed chlorine free. The World Bank has formally agreed to follow the recommended standards for paper usage set by Green Press Initiative—a nonprofit program supporting publishers in using fiber that is not sourced from Endangered Forests. For more information, visit www.greenpressinitiative.org.

In 2006, the printing of these books on recycled paper saved the following:

Trees*	Solid Waste	Water	Net Greenhouse Gases	Total Energy
203	9,544	73,944	17,498	141 mil.
'40' in height and 6–8" in diameter	Pounds	Gallons	Pounds Co$_2$ Equivalent	BTUs